The Marketing Planning Process

CIM Coursebook:
The Marketing Planning Process

Edited by: Phil Megicks

and

Authored by: Ray Donnelly
Graham Harrison

ELSEVIER

AMSTERDAM • BOSTON • HEIDELBERG • LONDON • NEW YORK • OXFORD
PARIS • SAN DIEGO • SAN FRANCISCO • SINGAPORE • SYDNEY • TOKYO
Butterworth-Heinemann is an imprint of Elsevier

Butterworth-Heinemann is an imprint of Elsevier
Linacre House, Jordan Hill, Oxford, OX2 8DP, UK
30 Corporate Drive, Suite 400, Burlington, MA 01803, USA

First published 2009

British Library Cataloguing in Publication Data
A catalogue record for this book is available from the British Library

Library of Congress Cataloging-in-Publication Data
A catalog record for this book is available from the Library of Congress

ISBN: 978-1-85617-716-0

For information on all Butterworth-Heinemann publications
visit our web site at www.elsevierdirect.com

Typeset by Macmillan Publishing Solutions
www.macmillansolutions.com

Printed and bound in Italy

09 10 11 12 13 14   10 9 8 7 6 5 4 3 2 1

Contents

Don't forget to look at the extra online support at www.marketingonline.co.uk which includes more free mini case studies.

Foreword

Hello and welcome to the CIM Coursebook for the Marketing Planning Process.

The focus of this unit is on the process of marketing planning and how it facilitates the shaping and implementation of marketing strategies to achieve organisational goals. In order to successfully pass the assessment in this unit, students will be expected to be able to display knowledge and understanding of the key aspects of marketing planning. In addition, they should be able to apply these to particular situations and evaluate the processes adopted in the formulation of marketing plans.

The approach to assessment will require candidates to develop a marketing plan in the context of a specific organisational setting which will need to focus on achieving the identified marketing objectives of that organisation in a particular scenario. Contextual application is therefore an essential aspect of enacting the marketing planning process that students must be able to address in different contexts and understand the implementation issues associated with this. Moreover, the way in which the process of marketing planning is applied in the selected context, and the tools, techniques, models, frameworks, theories and approaches are utilised in doing this need to be evaluated.

The highly practical nature of this unit requires a balance between theory and its application and it is important therefore that candidates acquire significant experience of understanding the way in which marketing planning is addressed in different organisation. Identifying examples of how the different stages of the planning process are undertaken and how marketing plans are developed is an important part of the learning associated with the unit. Although this text contains some illustrations of how this happens in the real world of marketing, further examples should be identified through researching different organisations in varying business settings. In particular, utilising information from their own organisation, or one with which they are especially familiar, is a good starting point for examples of marketing planning in practice.

The coursebook material comprises four sections, which broadly match up with the syllabus for the unit. The Section 1 covers essential content relating to marketing and marketing planning, their purpose within the organisation and how they relate to marketing strategy development in fulfilling organisational goals. The focus is therefore on the role of marketing within organisations, the purpose and process of marketing planning, the function and structure of marketing plans, and the fit with objectives at different levels of the organisation. Candidates should be able to examine marketing planning from the point of view of how it enacts marketing within organisations as an integrated process which provides strategic direction towards specific goals. It is important that students recognise that the level of this qualification is a step up from previous studies and requires evidence of an ability to explain, apply and evaluate the marketing planning process and its various dimensions. It is especially important therefore that a critical approach to the application of marketing planning and the development of plans is adopted, which takes account of the environment, resources, and objectives and practical implementation issues in a range of contexts.

In Section 2, the book addresses the topic of the marketing audit as a platform for proposing strategic outcomes. The sourcing of information which can be analysed to offer alternative strategic directions for the organisation is critical to the planning process in marketing and forms the basis for the subsequent setting of objectives, strategy formulation and its implementation. The book specifically considers the practicalities of undertaking a marketing audit, the process of auditing the marketing environment and analysis of the internal and external organisational environments.

In Section 3, marketing strategy formulation is approached through a detailed exposition of the segmentation, targeting and positioning approach. This provides the core of the marketing planning process which synthesises information from the audit in line with organisational goals and sets the strategy to define a detailed marketing programme that supports positioning in the markets targeted. Specific topics in the text relate to the process in defining marketing strategies, market segmentation techniques and evaluation, targeting approaches, and market positioning strategies. However, it is important to be cognisant of the holistic nature of this process, which should be addressed in an analytical manner drawing upon evidence to select appropriate target markets and formulate a complementary positioning for the identified customer groups.

The Section 4 addresses implementing marketing planning in practice with a specific emphasis on differences in achieving this in a range of organisational and market settings. In particular, the book concentrates on organisational structures, responsibilities, timescales and budgets for implementation. Further it considers barriers to implementing marketing planning and plans and ways of addressing these. Contextual aspects of implementation are then considered including the nature of the customer or product, the markets served, and the characteristics of the organisation and the goals it sets out to achieve.

The coursebook is designed to fully prepare candidates for their assessment and takes the reader through the requirements of the syllabus in a sequential way. It provides key learning points and relevant examples. These need to be supplemented by further reading and preparation in the application of theory using examples from different organisations. Additionally, students will benefit in terms of enhanced professional competence by systematically working through the material included, leading to greater knowledge of the marketing planning process and greater skills in its implementation in practice. We hope that you enjoy studying the unit and find the coursebook a useful resource in doing so.

Phil Megicks
Senior CIM Examiner – The Marketing
Planning Process
2009–2010

About the Authors

Phil Megicks is a Professor of Marketing and Strategy and Head of the School of Business and Management at the University of Plymouth. He is a Senior Examiner for the Marketing Planning Process unit of the new CIM Professional Diploma in Marketing. Phil has extensive experience of teaching and research in marketing education, and has authored a large number of referred articles and conference papers in the field of marketing planning and strategy particularly with regard to the small business and services sectors. He has also advised practitioners on how to address the realities of marketing planning using information based decision making approaches.

Ray Donnelly Author, trainer and academic who is also CIM Course leader, London Metropolitan Business School, London Metropolitan University.

Graham Harrison is a Chartered Marketer, Chartered Secretary and Consultant. He is also a Senior lecturer in London Metropolitan Business School, London Metropolitan University.

Marketing Planning to Deliver Marketing Strategies

The Different Roles of Marketing and its Cross-Functional Interaction Within Organisations

1.1　Critically evaluate the different roles of marketing and its cross-functional interaction within organisations

SYLLABUS REFERENCES

1.1:

- marketing as an organisational function and orientation
- marketing as a co-ordinating force in the organisation
- marketing's interface with other organisational functions
- exchange, transactions and relationships
- markets, customers, competition and value creation
- marketers as planners, strategists and tacticians
- marketing in theory and in practice

INTRODUCTION

This chapter covers the part of the syllabus which relates to the role of marketing, the relationship with other functional departments and the role of marketers.

The reader will be introduced to marketing as a function, an activity and as an orientation.

THE MARKETING FUNCTION

Marketing is the management process responsible for identifying, anticipating and satisfying customer requirements profitably. (Chartered Institute of Marketing)

According to Dibb et al. (2006) 'Marketing consists of individual and organisational activities that facilitate and expedite satisfying exchange relationships in a dynamic environment through the creation, distribution, promotion and pricing of goods, services and ideas'.

McDonald (2007) agrees there is considerable confusion about what marketing is.

He suggests that marketing is the process for:

- defining markets

- quantifying the needs of the customer groups (segments) within these markets

- determining the value proposition to meet these needs

- communicating these value propositions to all those people in the organisation responsible for delivering them, and getting their buy-in to their role

- playing an appropriate part in delivering these value propositions (usually only communications)

- monitoring the value actually delivered

There needs to be a clear distinction between marketing as an activity or business function and marketing as a concept, often referred to as a marketing orientation.

The marketing function is concerned with the management of the marketing mix, involving the various tools and techniques available to marketing managers. The marketing mix being, product, price, promotion and place (the four P's). Increasingly, the mix includes additional elements: people, physical evidence and processes (the extended services mix or seven P's). Depending on the organisation it can also involve the integrated planning of marketing together with any research that is undertaken into markets, customers, competitors, or on initiatives such as new products.

Marketing as a stand-alone function appears to have been transformed, replaced in an increasing numbers of organisations with marketing as a philosophy, i.e. a way of doing business that focuses on the customer. This could include sales, customer service, customer relationship management and customer intelligence, for example. Increasingly, a marketing orientation is seen as critical to the success of organisations, as it drives the organisation towards its goals through delivering value to customers.

MARKETING AS AN ORIENTATION

Kotler and Keller (2006) define the marketing concept as follows:

The marketing concept holds that the key to achieving organisational goals lies in determining the needs and wants of target markets and delivering the desired satisfactions more efficiently and effectively than the competition.

Organisations need to be marketing orientated, which means that there must be a clear focus throughout the organisation on customer needs and wants, and how these needs are met constantly.

Marketing orientation consists of five key aspects according to Narver and Slater (1990):

- Customer focus
- Competitor focus
- Integrated functional co-ordination
- Organisational culture
- Long-term profits

All of these aspects enable the business to, in theory, achieve sustainable competitive advantage through fulfilling customer requirements, and the cultural market orientation perspective is seen to be predominant in fulfilling this, particularly with regard to co-ordinating the organisation's resources.

A marketing orientation involves multiple departments or functions sharing information about customers and pursuing activities to meet customer needs and wants. An organisation that has a marketing orientation see the requirements of customers and potential customers as crucial and this drives all strategic decisions.

Kohli and Jaworski (1990) define market orientation in terms of three dimensions.

1. The generation of market information about the needs of customers and external environmental factors.

2. The dissemination of such information across organisational functions.

3. The development and implementation of strategies in response to the information.

Table 1.1	Different Business Orientations
Sales orientation	The emphasis is on selling more of the products and services they have to customers. Little attention is paid to identifying and satisfying customer needs and wants.
Production orientation	Maximising output to obtain economies of scale to maximise profits.
Product orientation	The emphasis is on the product, but ignoring customer tastes may result in product failures or lost market to competitors.

Similarly this intelligence-management approach enables the firm to fulfil the desires of customers in a way which leads it towards its aims and objectives.

There are three main alternatives to adopting a marketing orientation as shown in Table 1.1.

If a marketing orientation is to develop within organisations, attention should be given to each of the following:

- Create a customer focus throughout the business
- Listen to the customer
- Target customers precisely
- Measure and manage customer expectations
- Build customer relationships and loyalty
- Commit to continuous improvement
- Manage profitability
- Manage the marketing culture

MARKETING'S INTERFACE WITH OTHER ORGANISATIONAL FUNCTIONS

The complex nature of marketing means that there are many interfaces with other functional areas. Marketers in their own right cannot meet all the requirements of customers; they need to work with other parts of the organisation, especially where physical production processes are involved, and equally when people deliver intangible services.

Functional areas will each have their own concerns and constraints. Managers frequently find that those obstructing the implementation of marketing plans are not marketers themselves but staff from other functional areas. The marketing planner must take these concerns and constraints into account if plans are to be successfully executed.

Table 1.2	Organisational Conflicts Between Marketing and Other Functions	
Department	**Emphasis**	**Emphasis of marketing**
Production	Standard orders Long lead times Long runs	Customised orders Short lead times Frequent model changes
Inventory management	Economic stock levels Fast moving items Narrow stock range	Large stock levels Broad product range
Accounting	Standard transactions	Special terms and discounts
Finance	Firm budgets Price to cover total costs	Flexible budgets for changing needs Price for market growth
Credit	Lower credit risks Tough credit terms Tough collection procedures	Medium credit risks Easy credit terms Easy collection procedures

Decisions made by the marketing function will have repercussions on many other functional areas.

- A decision on a promotion, changing the credit terms, will have profound effects on credit collection and cash flow, concerns of the finance function.

- A promise by marketing to meet a delivery date will have implications on production in terms of production planning.

- Improvements in service delivery will depend on the co-operation and communication between the human resources and marketing functions.

Functional areas will have information that is of value to marketing and therefore a good relationship is essential to ensure the flow of information for decision making, monitoring and control.

The co-ordination and communication between marketing and the finance function is considered by many to be the most critical of all the functional relationships. Pricing will require costing information from the finance function. Performance measurement will require data from the finance function on promotional expenditure for future decision making.

An understanding of the areas of potential conflicts is useful as given in Table 1.2.

Marketing planning will require a co-ordinated approach with plans such as production, finance and personnel linking with the marketing plan.

A marketing orientation is only achieved when:

- departments engage in activities geared towards understanding customers' current and future needs;
- there is sharing of this understanding across departments;
- departments engage in activities designed to meet customer needs.

Market orientation requires organisation-wide generation, dissemination and responses to marketing intelligence. Marketing has a critical role in the co-ordination and communication between all of the functions.

ACTIVITY 1.1

Select an organisation that you are familiar with. Evaluate the relationship between marketing and the other functions, e.g. finance. What steps could be taken to improve the co-ordination and communication between departments? How will this lead to better value for customers?

MARKETERS AS PLANNERS, STRATEGISTS AND TACTICIANS

Marketing planning is a systematic process involving the assessment of resources and the marketing opportunities and threats. The marketing planning process requires marketers to take a critical planning perspective.

The marketing planning process enables information, aims and ideas to be developed into a document that can be easily understood, evaluated and implemented. The marketing planning outcome will be a plan for the future with objectives, strategies, identified resources and timings. Therefore, the plan acts as a 'road map' or blueprint for the organisation into the future.

Planners research, collect information, evaluate alternative courses of action and make decisions, whatever field the planner operates in. Marketers research the environment, both macro and micro. They collect information on customers and competitors. Alternative strategies are evaluated such as market penetration compared with market development. Decisions are made on strategies, marketing programmes, organisational structures and resourcing.

Marketers play a key role as strategists within organisations, asking and finding solutions to questions such as:

Which market should we be in?
How should we complete in this market?
What is the best way to deal with the threat of a new competitor?
How should we address changing consumer needs?

In military terms the strategist will seek the best way to deploy the resources available to win the battle. Furthermore, decisions will be made on when to concede ground and when to take offensive action to win the war. The marketer is faced with similar issues. If the organisational objectives are to be achieved then strategies will need to be formulated. However, just as with the military, changing circumstances will require changes in strategies if the objectives are to be achieved.

The marketer will formulate strategy to deal with the competitive threat; an offensive or defensive response. Should a frontal attack be used? Would a better strategy be to outflank the competitor by attacking selected segments of the market where the competitor is weak?

Marketers will also act as tacticians in day-to-day matters or operational matters. They will make short-term decisions on tactics within the longer-term framework provided by the marketing plan. In so doing they will address questions relating to operational matters such as:

How do we respond to competitor's price cut?
Should we use price competition or non-price competition?
Should this product be withdrawn?

These are all examples of tactical decisions.

MARKETING IN THEORY AND IN PRACTICE

The theory of marketing is relatively straightforward – customer focus, co-ordinating resources, competitive advantage, planning towards goals – all appear to be sound principles for any business or organisation to adopt. However the reality of marketing in the real world is much more difficult. As we will see as our investigation of the marketing planning process unfolds, putting it into practice involves a great deal of skill and knowledge, especially when encountering implementation issues in particular marketing contexts.

QUESTIONS

1. What advantages does the marketing orientation have over other organisational philosophies: product, production and sales?

2. Outline the benefits that a marketing orientation can offer the following organisations: a high-street retailer, a charity and a global fast-moving consumer goods brand.

SUMMARY

This chapter has introduced marketing as a function, activity and business orientation. The benefits of marketing as a way of doing business based on satisfying customer requirements have been outlined and the relationship of the marketing function with other business functions explored. Marketing success depends critically on the way the marketing concept is applied and how this translates into practical reality within organisation. Investigating how this achieved in a range of different organisational settings will be explored in the remainder of this text.

BIBLIOGRAPHY

Dibb, S., Simkin, L., Pride, W. and Ferrell, O.C. (2006) *Marketing: Concepts and Strategies*, 5th edition. Houghton Mifflin, Boston.

Kohli, A.K. and Jaworski, B.J. (1990) Market orientation: the construct, research propositions, and managerial implications. *Journal of Marketing*, 54(April), 1–18.

Narver, J.C. and Slater, S.F. (1990) The effect of a market orientation on business profitability. *Journal of Marketing*, 54(October), 20–35.

Kotler, P. and Keller, K.L. (2006) *Marketing Management*, 12th edition. Prentice-Hall, Englewood Cliffs, NJ.

McDonald, M. (2007) *Marketing Plans: How to Prepare Them, How to Use Them*, 6th edition. Butterworth Heinemann, London.

CHAPTER 2

The Synergistic Planning Process

1.2 Critically evaluate the synergistic planning process including the different components of the marketing plan and its links with delivering the organisation's corporate, business and marketing strategies

SYLLABUS REFERENCES

1.2:

- the purpose of marketing planning
- achieving a sustainable competitive advantage
- the stages of the marketing planning process: analysis, planning, implementation and control
- sequential, cyclical and iterative approaches to planning
- the outcomes of planning and plans
- contents of a marketing plan
- documentation and reality

INTRODUCTION

In this chapter, we are going to explore the marketing planning process. Why plan? What is the purpose of the marketing plan? What are the barriers? What should be included in a marketing plan? How do we obtain a competitive advantage from our planning?

The marketing plan contains the following stages:

- Mission, corporate goals and objectives
- Assessment of the current internal and external situation

11

- Internal analysis
- Segmentation, targeting and positioning
- Marketing strategy
- Tactical marketing plan
- Marketing budget
- Implementation and performance evaluation

In order to complete an effective marketing plan, all these sequential stages need to be undertaken.

THE SYNERGISTIC PLANNING PROCESS

Synergistic planning is the rational process of determining future actions based on a realistic consideration of the current situation and the outcome that is desired.

- Desired outcome
- Analysing the current situation
- Designing possible routes
- Deciding what to do and how to do it

The process of planning must start with a clear statement of what is to be achieved.

It is only when objectives are clearly defined that alternative courses of action can be evaluated and eventual success or failure measured.

Planning must take into account the current circumstances that will affect the achievement of the objective.

So the first step is to establish the current situation. It is important to establish the current strengths and weaknesses and identify the opportunities and threats for the future.

The next step is to analyse the information gathered and to generate potential strategies.

When a range of possible plans has been outlined, it then becomes necessary to go through a process of selection, normally by considering such factors as those below:

- Probability of success
- Resources required
- Acceptability of the proposed action and its implications
- Potential obstacles

The process of planning is not complete when a course of action has been chosen. It is essential to prepare detailed plans for all the groups and individuals involved, which must be integrated in such a way that all action undertaken supports the attainment of the overall objective through implementation of the plan.

Finally, performance measures and control mechanisms must also be established if the plans are to be successfully executed.

THE PURPOSE OF MARKETING PLANNING

McDonald (2007) defines the overall purpose of planning as follows:

The overall purpose of marketing planning and its principal focus is the identification and creation of sustainable competitive advantage.

McDonald states that marketing planning is necessary because of:

- Increasing turbulence, complexity and competitiveness
- The speed of technological change
- The need for the marketing planner to
  - identify sources of competitive advantage
  - force an organised approach
- The need for superiors to inform
- The need for non-marketing functions to get support
- The need for subordinates
  - to get resources
  - gain commitment
  - to set objectives and strategies

Organisations need a strategic marketing plan in order to adapt to changing business environments. Organisations must continually adapt and develop if they are to remain successful.

The marketing plan should provide a systematic framework with which to analyse the market place and supply a well-defined way to pursue strategic goals.

Drummond et al. (2008) summarises the reasons for planning as follows.

Adapting to Change

Planning provides an opportunity to examine how changes in the business environment have affected or will affect the organisation. It will enable management to focus on strategic issues as opposed to day-to-day operational problems.

Resource Allocation

No plan can succeed without appropriate resources. When a strategic perspective is taken, organisations are better placed to marshal the resources required to meet the strategic opportunities. Planning allows the organisation to deploy resources to meet threats and take advantage of opportunities.

Consistency

A marketing plan provides a common base to work from enhancing the decision-making process. The use of standard methods and formats should improve internal communication.

Integration

As a strategic process, planning should facilitate the integration and co-ordination of all marketing activities. Where there is a strategic focus, it should be possible to generate synergy from the individual elements of the marketing mix.

Communication and Motivation

The plan should clearly communicate strategic intent to employees and other stakeholders. Clear objectives and an understanding of the individual and group contributions to the process will serve to generate 'ownership' and motivation.

Control

All monitoring and control activities are based on some predetermined plan. The planning process should set meaningful targets and timescales, thus defining the criteria by which success is measured.

It is important to remember where the marketing plan fits into overall corporate strategy.

The corporate strategic plan and the marketing plan are not the same thing. The difference is largely of scope. The corporate plan has to consider all aspects of the organisation's business while the marketing plan is principally concerned with the marketing activities. The marketing plan is thus derived from the corporate plan. However, the marketing plan should be closely linked to the corporate plan and should support it.

Strategic decisions are concerned with:

- the long-term direction of the organisation;

- defining the scope of the organisation's activities in terms of what it will do and will not do;

Table 2.1   Differences between Strategic and Marketing Planning

Strategic planning	Marketing planning
Concerned with overall, long-term organisational direction	Concerned with the medium-term and the day-to-day performance
Provides a long-term framework for the organisation and the strategic business units	Concerned with one aspect of the organisation's development
Overall orientation needed to match the organisation to its environment	The functional orientation tends to be the main emphasis
Goals and objectives are evaluated from the perspective of the overall organisation	Goals and objectives are converted to specific targets
Emphasis on financial performance measures	

- matching the activities of the organisation to the environment in which it operates, so that it optimises the opportunities and minimises the threats;

- matching the organisation's activities to its resource capacity.

The differences between strategic and marketing planning are given in Table 2.1.

There are two types of marketing plan – the strategic and the tactical. The strategic plan takes a longer time frame and will provide a broad framework for the organisation's marketing activities.

Strategic marketing will focus on defining market segments and the positioning of products to obtain a competitive position. Plans will consider the changing business environment, changing market dynamics and the strategies and products of competitors. Broad strategies will be developed for distribution, product development, communications and pricing.

Tactical marketing takes a shorter time frame and will be concerned with day-to-day activities. The broad strategic marketing objectives and strategies will be developed into operational objectives and strategies. Problems are often repetitive and will deal with the individual aspects of the marketing mix such as pricing and promotions.

The differences between strategic and tactical marketing are given in Table 2.2.

ACHIEVING A COMPETITIVE ADVANTAGE

Marketing strategy and the concept of competitive advantage are intrinsically linked.

Table 2.2	Differences between Strategic and Tactical Marketing	
	Strategic marketing	**Tactical marketing**
Time frame	Long term	Short term
Focus	Broad	Narrow
Key tasks	Defining market and competitive position	Day-to-day operational marketing activity
Information and problem solving	Unstructured, external aspects	Structured, internal, repetitive
Examples	Market development, new product development	Promotions, price discounting

Source: Adapted from Drummond et al. (2008)

Competitive advantage is the process of identifying a fundamental and sustainable basis from which to complete. Marketing strategy aims to deliver this advantage in the market place.

Porter (1985) identified three fundamental sources of competitive advantage. These are:

1. Cost leadership
2. Differentiation
3. Focus

Let us examine each of these sources of competitive advantage, or generic strategies as they are called.

Cost Leadership

One source of competitive advantage is to pursue an overall cost leadership position. The focus of strategic activity is to achieve and maintain a low cost structure.

The organisation will be pursuing economies of scale, applying new technology, global sourcing of materials, minimising R&D expenditure and keeping a firm control of overheads.

Maintaining a competitive advantage through cost leadership can be difficult. Cost leadership with high volume will require high levels of investment. Better financed and resourced competitors may enter the market. Economies of scale may fall and overheads rise if market share is lost.

Differentiation

The product offered here is differentiated from the competition. The product offering must be perceived as unique. The source of differentiation should be on the basis of customer value and ideally should offer the opportunity for charging a price premium.

Maintaining a competitive advantage through differentiation can be difficult. The costs of differentiation can exceed the benefit of increased revenues. Differentiation and innovations may be replicated by competitors.

Common sources of differentiation include:

- Product performance
- Product perception
- Product augmentation

Focus

The aim is to specialise in specific market segments and develop detailed knowledge of customer requirements. This approach may be based on factors such as:

- Geographic area
- End-user focus
- Specialist products

Competitive advantage may be achieved by effectively meeting the needs of the chosen segments better than competitors. However, the advantage may be eroded as new competitors, perhaps better resourced and financed are attracted to profitable niches.

Michael Porter advises organisations to pursue competitive advantage through the adoption of one generic strategy and thereby avoiding the danger of 'stuck in the middle' positions which are perceived as having low profitability.

In order to be sustainable, the competitive advantage must be:

- Relevant – It must be appropriate to current and future market needs. It must also be relevant to the organisation – It must be achievable given the resources available to the organisation.

- Defensible – The competitive advantage must be difficult to replicate, otherwise competitors will simply copy.

So what are the barriers that prevent competitors from copying a successful formula? There are two major barriers.

1. Asset based barriers – These are tangible assets controlled by the organisation such as location, plant and machinery, finance and brands.

2. Skilled based barriers – These are skills and resources which utilise assets effectively and efficiently. Examples would include product design, quality management and brand development.

Table 2.3	Sources of Competitive Advantage
Source of competitive advantage	**Examples**
Product performance	Strong, easy to use, economic
Perception of product	Product positioning, brand image
Low-cost operations	Location, economies of scale, buying power
Legal advantage	Patents, copyright, contracts
Alliances and relationships	Networking
Superior skills	R&D, design
Flexibility	Customised solutions
Attitude	Focus on delivering value, innovation

Source: Adapted from Davidson (1997)

Davidson (1997) states that competitive advantage is achieved 'whenever you do something better than competitors. If that something is important to consumers, or if a number of small advantages can be combined, you have an exploitable competitive advantage'.

Davidson identified a number of sources of competitive advantage (Table 2.3).

ACTIVITY 2.1

Select an organisation that you are familiar with (this could be your own organisation). Identify any sources of competitive advantage that it has and how they were achieved. How can this be sustained over the longer term?

THE STAGES OF THE MARKETING PLANNING PROCESS: ANALYSIS, PLANNING, IMPLEMENTATION AND CONTROL

Marketing planning appears to be a simple logical step-by-step process. It is seen as a series of activities leading to the setting of marketing objectives and the formulation of plans for achieving them. However, in reality it is a multi-faceted, complex, cross-functional activity that touches on every aspect of organisations.

In small organisations the process may be informal but in larger organisations the process is likely to a formal system. Once started, marketing planning becomes part of the annual planning cycle.

The standard approaches to the planning process are:

Top–down: Senior management develop objectives and strategy which managers at an operational level then implement.

Bottom–up: Senior management devolves authority and responsibility for the formulation and implementation of strategy. Senior management then monitors the agreed objectives.

However, hybrid systems are also common, where the objectives are 'top–down' and the responsibility for formulation and implementation is devolved.

The stages of the marketing planning process are:

- Analysis
- Planning
- Implementation
- Control

Analysis: This covers the analysis of the marketing environment, both macro and micro, the industry, markets and competitor analysis.

Planning: This covers formulation of strategies and marketing programmes with the identification of resources and timing.

Implementation: This covers the practical execution of the plan, with any changes required to achieve this.

Control: This covers monitoring against planned targets, control mechanisms and performance metrics.

SEQUENTIAL, CYCLICAL AND ITERATIVE APPROACHES TO PLANNING

Marketing planning is a systematic process that involves assessing marketing opportunities and resources, determining marketing objectives and strategies, and developing marketing programmes and plans for implementation and control.

The marketing planning cycle is a circular process that runs in two directions, with planning running one way and feedback the other. There is a need for continuous feedback so that monitoring and control with modifications of the plan can take place (Figure 2.1).

Most organisations produce marketing plans each year. Once the system is up and running, the process will involve the revision of the previous year's plan, updating the marketing analysis and revising the strategies.

*The Marketing Planning
Cycle
Source: Dibb et al. (2006)*

OUTCOMES OF PLANNING AND PLANS

Planning is often seen as a restrictive process based on the programming of events and the generation of paperwork. Nothing could be further from the truth.

So what are the outcomes?

The outcomes of planning and the marketing plan are:

- A vision for the future of the organisation
- A mission to communicate
- Organisational objectives covering a range of time periods
- Objectives for each of the functional areas of the organisation
- Strategies to follow to pursue the objectives
- Identification of market segments
- Decision on which segments to target
- A positioning statement
- Plans for each element of the marketing mix with resources and timing:
  - product
  - place
  - price
  - promotion
  - people
  - physical evidence
  - processes

- Identification of performance metrics
- Identification of methods and times of monitoring
- Control measures
- Contingencies

The marketing plan should be a concise yet complete document setting providing a summary of the environment and the marketplace, the organisation's position together with the recommended strategy and detailed plans for the marketing mix.

The plan should be informative and must set out clearly the marketing activities that should be pursued to implement the desired strategy to achieve the organisational objectives.

The really successful marketing plan should be a vehicle for communication to managers throughout the organisation.

CONTENTS OF THE STRATEGIC MARKETING PLAN

So what does the strategic marketing plan look like? The content, structure, detail and complexity will vary from organisation to organisation. However, strategic plans tend to have common elements and the following components would be expected:

- External analysis
- Industry analysis
- Internal analysis
- Opportunity identification
- Objective setting
- Formulation of strategy
- Proposed marketing programmes
- Implementation and control

A typical structure for a marketing plan is shown below (adapted from McDonald, 2007):

1.0 Executive Summary
    1.1 Current position
    1.2 Key issues

2.0 Corporate Strategy
    2.1 Corporate mission/objectives
    2.2 Summary of overall position and corporate strategy

3.0 External and Internal Analysis
    3.1 Overview of market
    3.2 Competitor analysis

3.3 Future trends

3.4 SWOT

4.0 Marketing Objectives

4.1 Financial objectives

4.2 Marketing objectives

5.0 Marketing Strategy

5.1 Market segmentation

5.2 Competitive advantage

5.3 Marketing strategy

5.4 Specific marketing programme 7Ps

- Product
- Place
- Price
- Promotion
- Physical evidence
- People
- Processes

6.0 Implementation

6.1 Schedule of key tasks

6.2 Resource allocation

6.3 Budgets

6.4 Contingency

7.0 Control and Forecasting

7.1 Assumptions made in the plan

7.2 Critical success factors

- Benchmarks
- Metrics

7.3 Financial forecasts

- Costs
- Revenues

Whilst formats, conventions and content may differ, the key purpose of the strategic marketing plan is to generate action. The marketing planning process should address the critical issues of the organisation in a manner which is relevant to that individual organisation.

ACTIVITY 2.2

For an organisation of your choice, identify the assumptions that it should include in its plan and how they affect the detailed contents of the plan in practice.

BARRIERS TO PLANNING

We have seen that marketing planning is a logical sequence of steps and activities which lead to the setting of marketing objectives and the formulation of plans for achieving them. There are, however, many practical obstacles to be overcome. Many of the barriers to successful marketing planning are related to the human aspects of management.

While marketing planning has many clear benefits, it can create tension and barriers within the organisation. The newly defined strategies may create considerable change, involving new structures, systems, processes and even changes in staffing.

Culture: The prevailing culture may not be amenable to marketing plans. There is often resistance to change and a gradual return to the 'old practices'.

Power and politics: All organisations are subject to internal politics. The development of a strategic marketing plan may become a battlefield where vested interests fight over proposals, resources and status.

Analysis not action: Time and energy can be wasted by the process of analysing data and planning for action without actually taking any action. Many planning systems are more concerned with reviewing progress and controlling activities rather than tackling strategic issues.

Resource issues: A major aspect of the planning process is to match resources to strategic aims. Managers must take a realistic view of the resource position and endeavour to ensure resources are not needlessly withheld or overcommitted.

Skills: Managers may not have the skills to make the best use of the planning process and the opportunities for business development are missed opportunities.

McDonald (2007) identifies the following 10 principal barriers:

1. Confusion over marketing tactics and strategy
2. Isolating the marketing function from operations
3. Confusion between the marketing function and the marketing concept
4. Organisational barriers – the tribal mentality – failing to define SBUs correctly
5. Lack of in-depth analysis
6. Confusion between process and output
7. Lack of knowledge and skills
8. Lack of a systematic approach to marketing planning
9. Failure to prioritise objectives
10. Hostile corporate cultures

Whilst marketing planning may be considered a series of simple steps in practice the process is complex and challenging.

QUESTIONS

1. What is meant by the synergistic marketing planning process?

2. What are the contents of the strategic marketing plan?

3. How can differentiation assist in developing a competitive advantage?

SUMMARY

This chapter has explored the systematic marketing planning process and the nature of strategic marketing. It has identified the sources of competitive advantage as a basis for developing marketing strategies. The elements of a marketing plan are then considered and an overview of barriers to marketing planning presented.

BIBLIOGRAPHY

Davidson, H. (1997) *Even More Offensive Marketing*. Penguin Business, London.

Dibb, S., Simkin, L., Pride, W. and Ferrell, O.C. (2006) *Marketing: Concepts and Strategies*, 5th edition. Houghton Mifflin, Boston.

Drummond, G., Ensor, J. and Ashford, R. (2008) *Strategic Marketing Planning and Control*, 3rd edition. Butterworth Heinemann, Oxford.

McDonald, M. (2007) *Marketing Plans: How to Prepare Them, How to Use Them*, 6th edition. Butterworth Heinemann, Oxford.

Porter, M. (1985) *Competitive Advantage*. The Free Press, Collier Macmillan, London.

CHAPTER 3

The Role of the Marketing Plan in Relation to the Organisation's Philosophy

LEARNING OBJECTIVES

1.3 Critically evaluate the role of the marketing plan in relation to the organisation's philosophy and an organisation's strategic intent

SYLLABUS REFERENCES

1.3:

- the marketing plan as means of conveying organisational purpose and future vision
- the marketing plan as vehicle for setting direction and focus
- the marketing plan as an operational framework
- the marketing plan as a method of resource and budget allocation
- the marketing plan as a tool for performance measurement

INTRODUCTION

In this chapter, we will look at ways in which organisations attempt to communicate their purpose, through mission, vision and corporate values statements. A statement of the direction and purpose of the organisation is the key foundation on which objectives (see Chapter 4) and strategy (see Chapter 5) will be based. Many marketers argue that a marketing plan is incomplete without some reference to the organisation's mission or vision.

THE MARKETING PLAN AS A MEANS OF CONVEYING ORGANISATIONAL PURPOSE AND FUTURE VISION

The organisation's aims and aspirations are the results of a series of influences. Johnson et al. (2005) identify these as:

- Corporate governance – To whom should the organisation be accountable to? What is the regulatory framework within which executive decisions are made? These corporate governance issues relate to the accountability of the organisation and they exist to constrain management and protect the rights stakeholders.

- Stakeholders – These include groups such as shareholders, suppliers of finance, employees, suppliers, customers and the wider community. Organisations may try to further the interests of particular groups depending on the power and influence of such stakeholders.

- Business ethics – Ethics will affect the mission and the objectives of organisations. This will mainly shape the response to issues of corporate social responsibility.

- Cultural context – The cultural environment will influence the mission of the organisation. National cultures, organisational culture and individual employees will all have differing levels of influence on the organisational mission.

Stakeholders are able to influence purpose and strategies. However, power is shared unequally between the different groups of stakeholders. There are many different sources of power as shown in Table 3.1.

Table 3.1   Sources of Stakeholder Power

Within organisations	For external stakeholders
Hierarchy (formal power)	Control of strategic resources, e.g. materials, labour, money
Influence (informal power) e.g. charismatic leadership, control of strategic resources	Through internal links, e.g. informal influence
Possession of knowledge and skills e.g. finance specialists, computer specialists	Possession of knowledge or skills, e.g. subcontractors, partners
Control of human environment	Involvement in strategy implementation e.g. distribution outlets, agents
Involvement in strategy implementation	

Source: Adapted from Johnson et al. (2005)

The values, mission and objectives will be the result of a complex mix of negotiations and pressures from stakeholders who have varying degrees of power or influence.

The mission of the organisation is the unique purpose that distinguishes it from other organisations and defines the boundaries or scope of its activities.

Before writing a mission statement, the marketing planner needs to consider the purpose of the organisation. This involves asking questions such as:

- Why does the organisation exist:
  To create wealth for the owners?
  To satisfy the needs of stakeholders?
  To pursue some higher goal (scientific advancement)?
- What are the organisation's capabilities?
- What are the internal and external constraints?
- What are the current opportunities?
- What are the opportunities that might develop?

Bart and Baetz (1998) argue that a well-crafted mission statement has the following advantages:

- Provides direction
- Provides a basis for objectives and strategies
- Serves as a focal point
- Ensures unanimity of purpose
- Arouses positive feelings about the firm
- Resolves divergent views among managers

Clear mission statements play an important part in helping to frame marketing strategies. Poorly or wrongly defined mission statements can create strategic limitations which may result in loss of competitiveness and failure.

Pearce and David (1987) suggest that the mission statement should contain the following aspects:

- Customers (the target market)
- Products/services (offerings and value provided to customers)
- Geographic markets
- Technology
- Concern for survival/growth/profits
- Philosophy (organisation's values, ethics and beliefs)
- Public image (contribution to society/communities)
- Employees (importance of management and employees)
- Distinctive competence (how the organisation is better than or different from its competitors)

David and David (2003) undertook a study that found that many organisations failed to include many of the above aspects. Key areas of markets, technology, philosophy, public image and employees were frequently omitted or given little attention.

Mission statements that are very tightly defined may create problems in the future. As markets are evolving rapidly, a tightly defined mission may prevent the organisation developing a broader target market.

Mission statements provide a focal point and a sense of direction but many have been criticised for being too general ('to be the best') or over ambitious ('to be a global leader').

Greater emphasis is now being given to creating a vision. The vision is a picture of the organisation in the future, perhaps five years ahead. Wilson and Gilligan (2005) suggest that 'visioning' has been most successful where there has been clarity of managerial thinking in areas, including:

- The size of the organisation, business unit or brand in three to ten years time
- The corporate and brand values that will be developed
- The nature of the customer base and the customer segments that will be served
- How these customers should perceive the organisation or brand
- The geographic coverage that will have been achieved
- The overall position within the market and the competitive stance
- The links with other organisations

Hamel and Prahalad (1989) have discussed vision in terms of a strategic intent. They have defined strategic intent as involving the following:

- A dream that energises the organisation
- A long-term ambition which provides a sense of direction
- Offering a new goal for employees to work towards
- Provides coherence to the strategic plans
- Implying a stretch for the organisation

These authors argue that strategic intent requires a sizable stretch which will leverage the organisation's resources and capabilities. It is not sufficient to simply match resources with objectives. Strategic intent involves the setting of challenging goals that will stretch the organisation, requiring creativity to make the most of the limited resources.

In developing a vision, there is a need to understand both the organisation's competences and the future likely changes in the environment. There is also a need to understand the organisational values.

Organisations are now including statements on organisational values in their annual reports and other literature.

Values relate to the organisation's culture and the beliefs that are embedded within the organisation.

Values often include the principles of business:

■ Commitment to customers
■ Commitment to employees
■ Commitment to suppliers
■ Commitment to the environment
■ The ethical stance

Extract from the BT Vision, Strategy and Values Statement 2008

Our vision......

'is to be dedicated to helping customers thrive in a changing world. The world we live in and the way we communicate are changing, and we believe in progress, growth and possibility. We want to help all our customers and make their lives and businesses better with products and services that are tailored to their needs and easy to use.

This means getting ever closer to customers, understanding their lifestyles and their businesses, and establishing long-term relationships with them.

We're passionate about customers and are working to meet the needs they have today and innovating to meet the needs they will have tomorrow'.

Our values.....

'Our corporate identity defines the kind of company we are now and the one we need to be in the future.

Central to that identity is a commitment to create ways to help our customers thrive in a changing world.

To do this we must have brand values:

Trustworthy – We do what we say we will

Helpful – We work as one team

Inspiring – We create new possibilities

Straightforward – We make things clear

Heart – We believe in what we do

We are committed to contributing positively to society and to a sustainable future. This is part of the heart of BT'.

The vision provides a focus and direction for the organisation while the values provide guidance for the behaviour of management and employees.

ACTIVITY 3.1

Select an example of each of the organisations below and compare their mission, vision and value statements.

  a) a major retailer,

  b) an oil company,

  c) a construction company and

  d) a charity

THE MARKETING PLAN AS A VEHICLE FOR SETTING DIRECTION AND FOCUS

The marketing plan serves as a vehicle for setting the direction of the organisation and as a focus for the management and employees.

The marketing plan, incorporating a mission and vision, maps the direction the organisation should take both now and in the future. Management, having created the mission and vision, can then focus on specific objectives and strategies within a long-time framework. The statement of strategic intent, or mission, provides a reference point when making strategic decisions and when setting objectives. This should help to focus and prevent decisions which are not appropriate to the long term.

The marketing plan should be communicated widely if it is to provide the focus for both management and employees.

THE MARKETING PLAN AS OPERATIONAL FRAMEWORK

The marketing plan provides a framework for the operations of the organisation. Beyond the mission and the statement strategic intent, the marketing plan sets out plans for each aspect of the strategies to be pursued towards the organisational objectives.

The marketing plan identifies the objectives together with the strategies to be adopted to achieve those objectives at the different levels of the organisation. The marketing plan will outline the strategies and tactics for each area of the marketing mix.

The marketing plan provides a detailed route map for the different aspects of the marketing mix and provides guidance for other functional areas of the organisation, for example, production and human resources.

The marketing plan provides not only an effective route map for what should be done but also outlines how the organisation should monitor and control the implementation of the plan.

Milestones or points where reviews should be carried out are identified and the metrics to be used should be stated within a marketing plan.

Time is an important aspect of marketing planning. The marketing plan should identify the timing of the various activities. Organisations may be successful or could fail if the timing of various activities is not right. Critical issues are:

- Time to develop new products
- Timing and speed of entry into new markets
- Timing and speed of response to competitor challenges
- Timing of marketing communications

The marketing plan not only outlines strategies but also provides a detailed guide for the implementation of the plan, with activities, timing, resources and costs.

The marketing plan is not just some vague vision but a detailed plan for a range of activities that should be put into operation in pursuit of the organisational objectives.

THE MARKETING PLAN AS A METHOD OF RESOURCE AND BUDGET ALLOCATION

The marketing plan provides a basis for the allocation of resources and the allocation of budgets.

The marketing plan will identify activities to be carried out and should identify the resources required. The resources may be materials, equipment and labour or management time. Resources are always likely to be limited; therefore, the marketing plan provides an opportunity to consider priorities and those activities that are critical for the success of the organisation. Activities which are considered to be more important will receive a greater proportion of the resources.

Costs need to be calculated for each activity outlined in the plan. What is the cost of the internal marketing programme? What will that radio advertising cost? How much will the extra sales staff cost? What is the cost of that direct mail campaign?

The costs of all the activities should be incorporated into the marketing plan. Appropriate budgets should be allocated to the functional departments responsible for each aspect. Budget allocation requires strong negotiating skills, as politics within the organisation may conflict with the priorities set out in the marketing plan.

Responsibilities will need to be agreed and departments and individuals given authority to manage each delegated aspect of the master budget.

THE MARKETING PLAN AS A TOOL FOR PERFORMANCE MEASUREMENT

The marketing plan provides a tool which can be used to measure performance or progress with marketing activities.

A good marketing plan will identify not only the strategies and activities but also the milestones or times when they should be achieved by. When the plan is implemented the actual performance can be measured against the plan. Should the objectives not be achieved by the relevant milestones corrective action can be taken to put the plan back on track.

The marketing plan will identify various performance measures or metrics. At the corporate level, financial measures such as net profit, earnings per share and return on capital employed will be used. At a marketing level, metrics such as sales, conversion of enquiries to orders and customer retention will be used. Objectives for all of these will be set out in the plan and the actual performance can be measured at regular intervals to ascertain whether the required performance is being achieved.

The measures of performance can be used to compare performance between one period and another, typically one year with another. However, the performance measures can also be used to compare the performance of the organisation with other organisations and provide a basis for benchmarking.

QUESTIONS

1. How does a mission statement set direction and focus for
a) management and b) employees?

2. Select an organisation that you are familiar with. How could you use the marketing plan to allocate resources? What criteria would you use?

SUMMARY

In this chapter, we have seen how the marketing plan provides a direction and focus for the organisation and provides a statement of intent. The inclusion of mission, vision and values further sets the focus of the marketing planning process around essential outcomes and key aspects of the organisation's activities. The marketing plan also provides a 'blueprint' for organisational operations and a means of measuring the performance.

BIBLIOGRAPHY

Bart, C. and Baetz, M. (1998) The relationship between mission statements and firm performance: An exploratory study. *Journal of Management Studies*, 35(6), 823–53.

David, F.R. and David, F.R. (2003) It's time to redraft your mission statement. *Journal of Business Strategy*, 24(1), 11–14.

Hamel, G. and Prahalad, C.K. (1989) Strategic Intent. *Harvard Business Review*, 67(3), 63–76.

Johnson, G., Scholes, K. and Whittington, R. (2005) *Exploring Corporate Strategy*, 7th edition. Prentice Hall, Harlow.

Pearce, J. and David, F. (1987) Corporate mission statements: The bottom line. *Academy of Management Executive*, 1(2), 109–15.

Wilson, R.M.S. and Gilligan, C. (2005) *Strategic Marketing Management*, 3rd edition. Butterworth Heinemann, Oxford.

CHAPTER 4

The Relationship Between Corporate, Business and Marketing Objectives at an Operational Level and the Influences on Objectives

1.4 Evaluate the relationship between corporate, business and marketing objectives at an operational level and describe how they impact upon the activities associated with the marketing plan

1.5 Assess the external and internal influences on the formulation of objectives and specify the key environmental drivers of organisational change

1.6 Critically evaluate the wider impact of external and internal environmental forces on the setting of objectives at different levels and the process of planning marketing

1.4:

■ identifying a hierarchy of objectives
■ objectives at varying levels and timescales
■ different types of objectives: organisational, innovation, financial, market, relationship-focussed, societal, non-profit
■ consistency of plans with objectives
■ resource issues and constraints

1.5:

■ recognition of environmentally driven marketing planning and the resource-based view of the firm

- identify internal influences on objectives including objective setting process, corporate mission and strategy, culture, resources, capabilities
- identify external influences on objectives including economic conditions, markets, competition, industry life cycle, technological development
- identify drivers of organisational change including innovation, evolving consumer behaviour, globalisation, ethical consumption and corporate social responsibility, sustainability relationship management, stakeholder relations, globalisation

1.6:

- macro-environment: political, cultural, social, economic, technological, legal, ecological, ethical
- micro-environment: market, customers, competitors, industry structure and dynamics, suppliers, intermediaries
- internal environment: capabilities in functional areas, assets and core competencies, product and service portfolio, innovation, business relationships and strategic partnerships, current market position and past performance, dynamic capabilities, competitive advantage

INTRODUCTION

Having looked at the marketing plan as a means of conveying the vision and organisational purpose for the future, we will now look at how that vision can be translated into objectives.

Brassington and Pettit (2006) emphasise that 'marketing strategy cannot be formulated in isolation. It has to reflect the objectives of the organisation and be compatible with the strategies pursued elsewhere in the organisation'.

Marketers must therefore look at the corporate goals and objectives before developing their own strategies.

We will see later that objectives are influenced by many internal and external influences. Developing clear objectives is critical to ensuring the overall effectiveness of the organisation. Objectives are developed at different levels within the organisation and we will see that these form a hierarchy whereby objectives at each level are linked.

IDENTIFYING A HIERARCHY OF OBJECTIVES

A key issue when setting objectives is to remember to ensure they are relevant to achieving the corporate vision and mission.

Table 4.1	SMART Objectives
S Specific	Should be succinct and provide clarity as to what is to be achieved
M Measurable	Should identify targets that can be measured and monitored
A Aspirational	Should be challenging but achievable, and should motivate staff
R Realistic	Should be based on sound research. Should be achievable given the human, financial and other resources available
T Time-bound	A timescale should be set for the achievement of the objective for performance monitoring

Objectives are not only developed across a range of key areas, they also exist at a number of levels within an organisation. Objectives should cascade down through an organisational structure effectively forming a hierarchy. Objectives should be understood throughout the organisation and should be closely related to the organisation's resource capacity. The resource capacity will include the financial assets and facilities, human resources, production capacity, etc.

Setting objectives is an essential step in marketing planning and is central to developing effectiveness and competitive advantage.

Objectives are something you want to achieve. The objectives set should be SMART (see Table 4.1) if they are to be purposeful in directing the organisation towards corporate goals.

Corporate Objectives

Organisations will set primary or corporate objectives. At the corporate level management will be concerned with the overall long-term profitability and objectives are usually expressed in financial terms. For example:

- To achieve a 15% return on equity
- To increase operating profits by 20%
- To achieve a return on investment of 25%
- To achieve a return of 20% on capital employed (ROCE)
- To achieve growth of 10% in earning per share (EPS)

Functional Objectives

Objectives will be set for each functional area, operations, finance, human resources and marketing. Each functional objective developed for each function should be linked to the corporate objectives. Once the objectives have been developed, then strategies will be developed to achieve these objectives. For example:

Human Resources:

- To reduce staff turnover by 15% over the next 2 years
- To increase training by 5%

Finance:

- To reduce customer payment period by 12 days over the next 18 months
- To cut bad debts from 3% to 2% of turnover in next year

Operations:

- To increase labour productivity by 10% over the next 2 years

Marketing Objectives

Marketing objectives need to be developed to support the corporate objectives and to ensure the corporate objectives are achieved.

These marketing objectives will be mainly concerned with products and markets. Therefore, it is likely that the typical marketing objectives will concentrate on:

- Increasing sales of exiting products into existing markets
- Launching new products into existing markets
- Launching existing products into new markets
- Launching new products into new markets

These aims need to be developed into quantifiable and measurable objectives. These should be SMART – note each of the examples below is specific and there is a target date by which to achieve the objective. All of them must relate to the overall corporate objectives.

- To increase sales by 15% by 2011
- To increase market share of Product X by 10% by 2012
- To increase customer retention by 25% by 2012
- To increase the number of new products per year from 2 to 5 by 2012

Operational or Subsidiary Objectives

These will be related to the marketing mix. These will tend to be objectives that are more tactical. This area will have objectives related to the product mix, pricing or distribution aspects of the marketing mix.

Each subsidiary objective should be developed with the higher level marketing objectives in mind.

The whole idea of the hierarchy of objectives is that the organisation integrates and works together as a whole – there needs to be synergy if corporate goals are to be achieved.

The fictitious Garden and Leisure group, 'Town and City Gardens', illustrates the hierarchy of objectives (Table 4.2).

The hierarchy should ensure that objectives are developed at each level that should be consistent with the objectives at the level above. It is also essential that strong co-ordination is developed between functional areas. Poor co-ordination between functional areas may result in conflict which damages customer care.

In larger organisations there may be a range of strategic business units (SBUs) operating below the corporate holding company. These SBUs add another level to the hierarchy. SBU objectives will be derived from the corporate holding company objectives and the objectives will then cascade down to the functional level. These are often termed Business Level Objectives.

The use of the balanced scorecard framework to setting objectives (outlined later) is another possible approach to ensuring a balance of objectives is achieved.

OBJECTIVES AT VARYING LEVELS AND TIMESCALES

In today's marketing environment, it is becoming increasingly difficult to have a predetermined plan for the long term. The changing economic

Table 4.2 Hierarchy of Objectives

	Objectives	Strategy
Corporate 2009–2012 (over 3 years)	Increase operating profit by 25%	By increasing market share to 20% in regional market
Marketing 2009–2012 (over 3 years)	Achieve 20% market share of regional garden and leisure market	By providing best range of products to key market segments By providing high service standards Promote effectively
Marketing mix		
Product	Provide wide range of products for key market segments	Upgrade centre facilities with restaurants and advice booths
Promotion	Create awareness of the garden and leisure centres	Re-launch centres after refurbishment
Physical evidence	Create an environment which conveys quality	Develop display gardens and professional signage
Service	Provide excellent service	Retrain staff

Source: Adapted from Drummond et al (2008)

Table 4.3	Planning Timescale Horizons
Typical planning horizons	
Short term	1–3 years
Medium term	3–5 years
Long term	5 years and beyond

environment, shortening of product life cycles and dramatic advances in technology have made long-term planning difficult. Most organisations will prepare marketing plans for the medium term within a framework of less-detailed longer term objectives or vision for the future (Table 4.3).

Long-term objectives are set for planning horizons of up to 5 years ahead. Shorter term objectives are set which fit with the overall direction of the longer term objectives. These short-term objectives are likely to be associated with driving operational activities.

Target and budgets will be set based on the short-term objectives for monitoring and control.

It is essential that the short-term objectives and the operational targets and budgets are closely linked with the long-term objectives.

DIFFERENT TYPES OF OBJECTIVES

Objectives will vary from organisation to organisation. There will be differences between the different organisations that exist.

Organisations in the for-profit sector will set a range of financial objectives. These financial objectives will include:

- Operating profit
- Earnings per share
- Dividends per share
- Return on investment
- Return on capital employed
- Debt to equity

Organisations may set organisational objectives which are related to markets. Typical objectives set include:

- Market share growth
- Market share maintenance
- Share of product market
- Share of market segment
- Establishing a market position in a new market

Organisations increasingly need to innovate and learn. Typical objectives set in this area include:

- Number of new products introduced
- Products patented
- Time to market

In the not-for-profit charitable sector objectives will reflect the desire to enhance the quality of lives. Typical objectives include:

- Raising funds
- Raising awareness
- Control of costs related to funds raised
- Number of clients supported
- Targeting key influencers

The objectives of 'Brake', the road safety charity, illustrate the range of objectives set by charitable organisations.

BRAKE – THE ROAD SAFETY CHARITY

To raise awareness among citizens – children and adults – of the extent of death and injury on roads and their power to prevent it through careful use of the roads

To stimulate community activities promoting road safety, involving volunteers and professional bodies

To target key high-risk groups to achieve behavioural improvements on roads by providing research-based road safety educational projects, including in the following sectors as priority: fleet drivers, company risk managers, young drivers, parents and children, particularly in deprived communities

To contribute to the professional development of road safety practitioners

To drive forward road safety policy at central and local government levels and through a research-based agenda

To work in partnership with other road safety providers

To work in partnership with other road safety providers to ensure innovation and economy in all projects

Source: Extract from the objectives of Brake

This does make the measuring of achievement difficult, as marketers are used to dealing in measures such as units or money. However, charities and not-profit-making organisations start their marketing activities with a set of clear objectives.

Charities may also have commercial activities such as shops where funds are raised from the sale of goods donated. These charities will have a range of financial objectives related to those activities as well as objectives related to the main purpose of the charity.

ACTIVITY 4.1

Select an organisation with which you are familiar and develop a set of objectives at different levels from corporate through to specific marketing outcomes over different timescales.

THE BALANCED SCORECARD

There is a link between the setting of objectives and the identification and setting of performance measures which will be needed for implementation, monitoring and control. The balanced scorecard (Kaplan and Norton, 1992) takes an approach which closely links objectives and performance measures.

Kaplan and Norton suggested that a balanced set of objectives should be prepared with performance measures developed alongside at the same time.

Central to the balanced scorecard approach is the view that management should be able to look at the business from four key perspectives shown in Table 4.4.

Traditional financial measures have encouraged a bias towards the short term. Research and development, customer service and training are often cut back to improve annual financial reports, with long-term consequences on profitability and growth.

The balanced scorecard provides managers with a more holistic view of the business than is provided by financial measures alone. Managers are required to develop clear objectives with performance measures. The process forces managers to understand the relationships between functional departments of the organisation improving the prospect of consistency between objectives.

Table 4.4	Balanced Scorecard Perspectives
Customer perspective	How do customers see the business? Objectives and performance measures prepared from the customer's perspective (e.g. time, service, quality and performance) will be needed.
Internal perspective	What are the critical internal processes that will enable the organisation to meet customer needs?
Innovation and learning perspective	What is the innovation capability of the organisation? Is the organisation capable of learning?
Financial perspective	The view of the organisation from the shareholders point of view.

Table 4.5 shows a range of objectives with associated measures using the balanced scorecard approach.

CONSISTENCY OF PLANS WITH OBJECTIVES

It is inevitable that organisations will experience conflicts when setting objectives. These problems are likely to be compounded when multiple objectives are set. For example, it is impossible for an organisation to satisfy objectives of maximising both sales and profitability at the same time. Likewise objectives of risk aversion with rapid growth are incompatible.

Table 4.5	Measuring Balanced Scorecard Perspectives
Strategic objectives	**Strategic measures**
Financial	
F.1 Return on capital	→ ROCE
F.2 Cash flow	→ Cash flow
F.3 Profitability	→ Net margin
F.4 Profitability growth	→ Volume growth rate vs. industry
F.5 Reliability of performance	→ Profit forecast reliability
	→ Sales backlog
Customer	
C.1 Value for money	→ Customer ranking survey
C.2 Competitive price	→ Pricing index
C.3 Customer satisfaction	→ Customer satisfaction index
	→ Mystery shopping rating
Internal	
I.1 Marketing	→ Pioneer percentage of product portfolio
▪ Product and service development	
▪ Shape customer requirement	
I.2 Manufacturing	→ Hours with customer on new work
▪ Lower manufacturing cost	
▪ Improve project management	→ Total expenses per unit vs. competition
I.3 Logistics	→ Safety incident index
▪ Reduce delivery costs	
▪ Inventory management	→ Delivered cost per unit
I.4 Quality	→ Inventory level compared to plan and output rate
	→ Rework
Innovation and learning	
IL.1 Innovate products and services	→ Percentage revenue from pioneer products
IL.2 Time to market	→ Cycle time vs. industry norm
IL.3 Empowered workforce	→ Staff attitude survey
IL.4 Access to strategic information	→ Strategic information availability
IL.5 Continuous improvement	→ Number of employee suggestions

Source: Adapted from Kaplan and Norton (1992, 1993)

There are a range of strategic trade-offs facing organisations:

- Profit margins versus competitive position
- Profit goals versus non-profit goals
- Growth versus stability
- Short-term profitability versus long-term growth
- Penetration of existing markets versus development of new markets
- Growth versus stability
- Risk avoidance versus risk taking

These mean that the marketing planner must decide between the trade-offs if objectives are to provide useful goals.

There is a further challenge for the marketing planner. If plans are to be successfully executed, it is critical that the strategy and tactics outlined in the plan are consistent with the objectives set.

An objective related to raising quality standards would be inconsistent with marketing programmes including promotions and price reductions.

RECOGNITION OF ENVIRONMENTALLY DRIVEN MARKETING PLANNING AND THE RESOURCE-BASED VIEW OF THE FIRM

The foundation of any marketing plan is the organisation's mission and vision statement.

The mission statement will be based on careful analysis of existing and forecasted environmental conditions and the resources, competences and technology of the organisation.

This matching of internal strengths and weaknesses with external opportunities and threats leads us to two views of the organisation:

- The market orientation view – an outside-in perspective
- The resource-based view – an inside-out perspective

Market orientation refers to the way the organisation implements the marketing concept. The marketing environments will be analysed, both macro and micro. The market will be analysed and competition identified. The customers' current and future needs will be analysed.

In the market orientation view there is a deep knowledge of the competition from the point of view of the customer – effectively demonstrating the outside-in perspective. Without this understanding the organisation is vulnerable to attack from new and unexpected sources of competition.

Market orientation emphasises responsiveness to market needs and superior performance related to market intelligence.

The marketing process is seen as cross-functional and not simply the domain of the marketing department. We should remember that an organisation's marketing orientation is not the exclusive responsibility of the marketing department; intelligence gathering should be the concern of all functional areas.

In contrast the resource-based approach takes the view that superior performance is dependent on historically developed unique or distinctive resources.

The resource-based approach identifies the need for the organisation to develop capabilities that are unique to it. Resources are the organisational capabilities and competences that will lead to the development of competitive advantage if they match the opportunities available in the external environment.

Types of resources:

- Technical resources: These include the technology development and product development functions. This term covers access to research, information systems and processes as well as personal skills of staff.

- Financial standing: This covers the ability of the firm to attract capital and invest it to exploit opportunities. Firms are funded by a mix of debt and equity and the balance between these and the investment yields achieved are critical to the long-term well-being of the organisation. Financial standing will determine whether an organisation can raise capital and at what rate.

- Managerial skills: Firms require strategic management skills to succeed in their chosen environment. One reason that firms sometimes suffer when a 'shock' occurs in their environment is that the management skills required to assess the event, consider the options and take action are not up to the challenge. The recession of 2009 will test the managerial skills of many organisations.

- Organisation: The organisation has a range of organisational resources such as processes, systems, collective skills and a culture that can provide a strong basis for competitive advantage.

- Information systems: Information about the state of the environment and the organisation are crucial for making appropriate decisions. If an organisation is scanning its environment for opportunities and knows the availability and cost of specific resources, it will be in a stronger position to exploit this information over a competitor that does not have the information.

- An alternative view of organisational competences is to link them to specific processes of the organisation – strategic operations or departmental competences.

For a resource to be considered a valuable capability or core competency, it needs to pass two tests:

- It should meet the needs of the business environment
- It should be difficult for the competition to reproduce

In markets where products have become commodities, the skill in developing competitive advantage is derived from the organisation's ability to combine a series of capabilities such as operational efficiency and speed of delivery.

The resource-based view emphasises the need for the organisation to exploit the distinctive capabilities it has. In contrast the market-orientated view emphasises the need to be responsive to changes in the marketing environment.

INTERNAL INFLUENCES ON OBJECTIVES

There are a range of internal influences on the organisation that management will be aware of when setting objectives:

1. Internal stakeholder expectations

    - *Shareholders* will be interested in the profitability of the organisation. They will expect to see rising profits each year. Institutions and individual shareholders also expect dividends to be paid and expect to see rising dividends per share over the years. Objectives and strategies will be watched to ensure the organisation is not engaging in high-risk projects

    - *Employees* will be interested in job security and the potential for increased earnings

    - *Trade Unions* will be interested in protecting the jobs, employment conditions and pay of their members

2. Management style

    - Attitudes to risk will influence whether objectives are low risk or high risk

    - Attitudes to growth will influence objectives, for example organic versus acquisition

3. Organisation culture

   ▪ Is the organisation responsive to change?
   ▪ Is there a culture of innovation?

4. Internal resources

   ▪ Financial: Poor cash flow will have impact on objectives selected
   ▪ Staffing: A lack of skilled staff may encourage an objective of outsourcing

EXTERNAL INFLUENCES ON OBJECTIVES

The Macro-Economic Environment

Political, economic, social and technological changes will all influence the objectives set by management. Some examples are as follows.

Political pressure has resulted in organisations setting objectives related to the environmental impact. The 'carbon footprint' energy-use objectives of all businesses, for example those related to reducing the use of plastic bags by supermarkets, are the result of political pressure.

The economic recession of 2009 is likely to have a profound impact on the setting of new objectives and the formulation of new strategies for the next 1–5 years. Therefore objectives related to survival, cash generation, cost reductions are likely to replace objectives for growth.

The Micro-Economic Environment

Competition within influences the types of objectives set by management. Intense competition in the automobile manufacturing sector results in objectives aimed at maintaining or increasing market share. Some examples are as follows.

Customers' buying behaviour is changing with the impact of the Internet and will influence the objectives set by management.

External stakeholders influence the objectives of organisations to varying degrees. These include:

▪ General public: General public will have expectations of organisations and public opinion may influence the objectives.

▪ Pressure groups: Environmental pressure groups, such as Friends of the Earth, Greenpeace will lobby for changes in the objectives of organisations.

▪ Government and regulators: Expectations of Government and regulators will influence objectives. The 2008–2009 credit crunch, has resulted in regulators bringing pressure to bear on financial services organisations which are likely to influence future objectives especially those related to risk.

DRIVERS OF ORGANISATIONAL CHANGE

All organisations are influenced by increasing levels of change. We can study change from two perspectives:

- Cyclical change: A variation that is repetitive and often predictable (seasonal variations or changes in business activity)

- Evolutionary change: A fundamental shift which is often sudden

Whichever type of change occurs, it will have consequences on strategy formulation. Change should be seen as a natural consequence of the business environment and therefore should be an accepted part of strategic development.

Drummond et al. (2008) suggest that the following questions regarding change should be asked:

- What drives change?
- How does change impact on our markets?
- How does change impact on our business environment?
- What is the result of change on the organisation's strategy?

So what are the key drivers of change?

The starting point should be the use of the PESTEL framework, which is a useful tool for examining the business environment. Changes are being driven by the following factors:

Political

- The changing political landscape of Eastern Europe
- Increasing power of economies such as China and India
- The enlargement of the European Union

Economic

- Downturn in the global economy
- Threats of inflation turning to threats of deflation
- Changes in the savings/debt ratio

Social

- Demographic trends such as falling birth rates, an ageing population and migration

- Greater social mobility
- Higher levels of education

Technological

- Convergence of technologies
- Growth of biotechnologies

Environmental

- Industry effects on climate change
- Reduced stocks of natural resources

Legal

- Trade restrictions and competition
- Safety standards and consumer protection

Globalisation over the last 20 years has led to the emergence of transnational segments of consumers with similar demands. Complex interactions now occur between organisations across the globe. Companies are changing business models and structures to take advantage of different costs of production in different locations and markets.

Corporate Social Responsibility (CSR) has emerged as an essential ingredient in business. CSR relates to actions which are above and beyond that required by law.

As well as all aspects of social responsibility towards their customer's organisations are also expected to be:

- Socially responsible towards the environment
- Socially responsible in employee relations
- Socially responsible towards the wider community

Other dimensions of CSR include:

- Stakeholder relations: There is increasing pressure on organisations to engage more widely with stakeholders.

- Ethical consumption: Consumers are increasingly concerned at the sourcing of products and wish to purchase from businesses that have ethical credentials.

- Innovation: Shorter product life cycles have increased the pressure on organisations to pace a greater emphasis on creativity and innovation.

Other drivers of organisational change include:

- Disintermediation: The growth of the Internet has reduced the need for intermediaries

- Mass customisation: Customers can order bespoke products and these can be produced with similar efficiency to mass produced goods (Table 4.6)

- Outsourcing and off-shoring: This has become common for many organisations as pursue lower costs

- Fragmentation of media: Digital TV, proliferation of TV and Internet channels.

- Data mining: Increased information about customers available for segmentation and targeting customers.

- Impending shortages of raw materials

- Increasing energy costs

- Increasing levels and costs of pollution

- Concerns over environmental change and global warming

- Increased cynicism over marketing

What are the impacts of these changes?

- Demographic patterns mean traditional markets are becoming more challenging

- Consumer habits are changing

- Change is accompanied with intense competition

- Incremental growth rates of the past are likely to be replaced by more volatile patterns in future

- Shorter product life cycles will mean less time to recover investment in those products

- Greater difficulty predicting the future

What are the results of these changes?

- Strategies of the past do not guarantee success in the future.

- Markets will need to be redefined for the future.

- New strategies will need to be developed to cope with the new circumstances.

Organisations that are marketing-orientated, flexible and with an understanding of customer needs will survive. Many organisations will not survive as they do not have the capability to predict and cope with change.

Table 4.6	Drivers of Consumer Change
Changing demographics	■ Youthful elderly: better health and fitness and with more money than previous generations ■ Ageing children: exposed to technology and media with strong brand awareness ■ Changing family relationships: fewer set life stages ■ Smaller household size
Cash-rich/time Poor segment	■ More single households ■ Over 70% of women work
The 24-hour Society	■ Internet growth ■ Home delivery
The search for greater value	■ Greater price awareness (driven by Internet) ■ Emphasis on quality in price/value relationship
Ethical consumerism	■ Fair trade ■ Buyers with conscience ■ Greater cynicism over marketing claims
Health and healthy lifestyles	■ Alcohol and tobacco health risks ■ Low-sugar, low-fat products ■ Fitness clubs

Such ability to be dynamic in response to change is a key factor in organisational success, and is one of the important aspects of internal capability that needs to be factored into the marketing planning process. This dimension of the internal environment, along with other organisational factors will be considered in more detail in the next section of this book.

QUESTIONS

1. What is meant by the hierarchy of objectives?

2. What are the key drivers of organisational change in a) the international passenger air travel industry, b) the food and grocery retail sector, c) the fashion clothing industry?

SUMMARY

This chapter has considered the influences on the development of objectives, both internal and external. Objectives are developed at different levels of the organisation and for different time periods. The main drivers of organisational change are then examined and their effects on objectives and the marketing planning process are considered.

BIBLIOGRAPHY

Brassington, F. and Pettit, S. (2006) *Principles of Marketing*, 4th edition. Pearson Education, Harlow.

Drummond, G., Ensor, J. and Ashford, R. (2008) *Strategic Marketing Planning and Control*, 3rd edition. Butterworth Heinemann, Oxford.

Kaplan, R.S. and Norton, D.P. (1992) The Balanced Scorecard: Measures that Drive Performance. *Harvard Business Review*, 70(1).

Kaplan, R.S. and Norton, D.P. (1993) Putting the Balanced Scorecard to Work. *Harvard Business Review*, 71(5).

Senior Examiner's Comments – Section One

On completion of Section 1, students should have a detailed knowledge and understanding of:

- The role of the marketing function within organisations and how it interfaces with other organisational functions

- The purpose of marketing planning and the stages of the marketing planning process

- The different ways in which a marketing plan can contribute to an organisation

- The nature and relationship between organisational objectives at different levels

- The factors that influence the setting of objectives at different levels within organisations

In addition students are expected to be able to apply this knowledge to practical marketing planning situations across a range of different organisational settings including consumer and business goods and services, profit- and non-profit oriented organisations including the public sector, and large as well as small and medium sized enterprises. Examples from local, national, international and global markets should be used to distinguish similarities and contrasts in marketing planning behaviour around the proposed models studied.

The critical requirement of the unit is the ability to examine the implementation of marketing planning in practice through recognition of how it is undertaken by different organisations. Furthermore, students need to be able to evaluate the validity of the marketing planning process as well as its constituent stages in directing organisations toward their goals, and critically assess the contribution of the plethora of concepts, models and frameworks employed.

The Marketing Audit and Strategic Outcomes

CHAPTER 5

The Practicalities of Undertaking a Marketing Audit

LEARNING OBJECTIVES

2.1 Critically evaluate the practicalities of undertaking a marketing audit including resource limitations and implications within the organisational context
2.2 Assess the concept of the organisation as an open system faced with changing environmental conditions and internal capabilities

SYLLABUS REFERENCES

2.1:
- conducting a marketing audit in practice
- scope, timing and frequency
- responsibility and objectivity
- constraints and issues

2.2:
- complex and dynamic external environment
- variability in organisational resource, asset and competence base
- controllable and uncontrollable influences
- responding to external and internal change
- shaping strategy and plans proactively

INTRODUCTION

This chapter looks at the practicalities of conducting a marketing audit covering both the internal and external dimensions and its importance as part of the marketing planning process. In particular, we will identify the process of the audit and how it should be undertaken in practice.

THE MARKETING AUDIT

Having already looked at the main elements of the marketing planning process, we will now look at the foundation of marketing planning and plans, the marketing audit.

Kotler et al. (2008) suggests organisations continually need to ask themselves for four key questions:

1. What business are we in?
2. What are we in business for?
3. Who are our customers?
4. What sort of business are we?

We will see later when we examine the concept of segmentation, knowing the business we are in, helps define future direction. Is Ryanair in the airline business or the transport business?

> If you want to travel from London to Manchester, you can choose from the train, coach, car or aeroplane, so what business should Ryanair be in?

Clearly understanding why the organisation is in business gives it focus and knowing exactly who its customers are enables it to concentrate on satisfying their needs. Who are the customers for a university? The students who are being taught, their parents who may be paying for them, the recipients of research services and the wider community, or potential employers?

WOOLWORTHS

For almost 100 years, it has offered everything for house and home, from kitchenware and tools, to haberdashery and toys.

Generations of teenagers popped in for CDs and some "pic 'n' mix" sweets on their way out.

However, nostalgia might not be enough to sell a brand which, in the past, had identified itself by value, convenience and reliability.

Giles Lury, brand consultant at The Value Engineers, believes that Woolworths' business model lacked clarity and vision, and this had an immediate impact on its brand.

'Woolworths had a great role as a generalist. But a lot of their market area moved to other suppliers. It tried to be a jack-of-all trades, but it lost out to those who were masters of one', he says.

'Woolworths was left with no answers when faced with stiff competition from supermarkets and internet retailers,' adds Amy Frengley, senior consultant at Brandsmiths.

'Its original demographic has become much more sophisticated. Certainly they have new expectations, shaped in part by other retailers, as to what a store like Woolworths should be delivering even within the parameters of a low-price retailer'.

Woolworths closed its doors at the start of 2009.

What sort of business are we, in? is therefore a crucial question. Porter's generic strategy model suggests an organisation has three positions it can take in the market; cost leadership, differentiation and stuck in the middle. Being stuck in the middle is the position to be avoided as customers find it difficult to understand exactly what they can expect from the organisation. Woolworths found itself 'stuck in the middle' and paid the ultimate price by going into administration and eventually closing down its stores in 2009.

The marketing audit has three purposes (Wilson and Gilligan, 2005):

1. Identifying the organisations current market position

2. Understanding the environmental opportunities and threats it faces

3. Clarifying the organisation's ability to cope with environmental demands

WHAT IS AN AUDIT?

A marketing audit is a systematic review and appraisal of the environment and the company's operations.

Kotler and Keller (2006) suggest an audit is:

A comprehensive, systematic , independent and periodic examination of a company's or business unit's marketing environment, objectives, strategies and activities with a view to determining problem areas and opportunities and recommending a plan of action to improve the company's performance.

Organisations do not operate in a vacuum but as part of a wider environment (Figure 5.1).

The audit is central to the planning process and supports the corporate and marketing decision-making process; it helps the organisation understand where it is now, where it wants to be and how it will get there. It is the key to the marketing planning process, particularly from the point of view of formulating strategies.

The marketing audit can be split into two parts: internal and external. According to Kotler and Keller (2006), it should comprise the following six components(Table 5.1).

The marketing environment audit relates to the external environment, and the remaining five components relate to the internal environment. Information on both external forces and internal capabilities are required if an organisation is going to develop effective marketing plans.

Figure 5.1 highlighted the key aspects of the external environment which consists of political, economic, social, technological, environmental

FIGURE 5.1

*Levels of the Marketing
Environment*

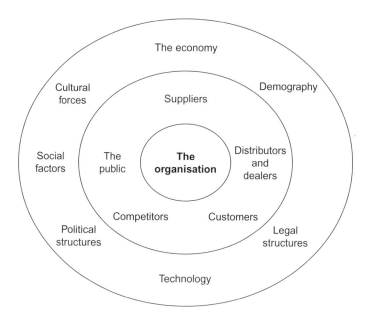

Table 5.1 Components of a Marketing Audit

Marketing environment	Analysis of the major macroeconomic forces and trends together with actors in the microenvironment including customers, competitors, distributors and suppliers amongst others (see Figure 5.1)
Marketing strategy	Review of the organisations marketing objectives and strategy to check on their suitability for the current conditions
Marketing organisation	Understanding the structural capability of the organisation and how well suited it is for the current or future conditions
Marketing systems	Evaluate the organisations systems for analysis, planning and control of the marketing plan
Marketing productivity	How well are the individual components of the marketing plan performing and how cost effective are they? Are alternative or more cost effective methods available?
Marketing functions	Each element of the marketing mix should be evaluated

and legal influences (PESTEL). It also embraces, customer influences, competition and suppliers. All of these factors influence the organisation but cannot control them i.e. it has to respond to them. They are generally considered to be outside the control of an organisation.

The microenvironment comprises customers, competitors, suppliers, distributors, dealers and the public. These factors are also external to the organisation and are seen to be influenced in their behaviour by the wider external forces of the macroenvironment. Assessing the microenvironment is critical to developing competitive marketing strategy that takes account of consumer behaviour, competitor activity and the role of intermediaries as well as suppliers and the general public as stakeholders in the markets that the organisation is involved in.

The internal environment of the organisation must be audited to identify its current position and assess its particular competences and short-comings in the light of the markets it serves and the competition that it is faced with.

FREQUENCY OF AN AUDIT

The actual intervals which an audit should take place in will depend on the:

- nature of the business being conducted
- rate of environmental change taking place
- duration or length of the organisations planning cycle

In a fast moving market, such as technology, it is essential to ensure the organisation stays ahead of the competition and a frequent audit gives strength to the planning process. Equally the organisation's marketing environment can be changing rapidly, or unexpectedly; consider the severe economic changes which took place in 2008, for example. Organisations needed to have the structures in place to manage these difficulties, which had an impact on most business sectors.

Finally, most organisations will have an annual or rolling planning cycle, and the preparations for the planning cycle are usually the trigger to commence an audit.

Key areas within the organisation can then be reviewed on a flexible but timetabled basis.

When conducting an audit, most commentators would agree that a logical and consistent approach is more effective as comparisons can be made with earlier audits to demonstrate improvements within the process. The generic stages are shown in Table 5.2.

Not all organisations conduct an audit, despite evidence to suggest that organisational performance is improved where an audit is conducted. Wilson and Gilligan (2005) suggest that those organisations that do carry out audits tend to wait until things go wrong i.e. fire fight rather than be proactive. This leads to a short-term reaction characterised by the rapid introduction and withdrawal of products.

Table 5.2	Stages of a Marketing Audit
1. Preaudit	Here the scope or terms of reference of the audit are agreed and circulated
2. Information/data collection	The information to be collected is identified which *inter alia* could include channel data, pricing, markets and market structure and the environment
3. Data analysis	Data which has been collected is now analysed. This will set out (for example) the industry standards and the organisation's own performance in relation to that standard
4. Recommendations	Recommendations arising from the data analysis are now made
5. Implementation programme	Findings/recommendations from the audit should be circulated and implemented to key managers within the organisation

Fire fighting (crisis management) may produce results for the organisation, but it does not address any fundamental problems which may be inherent within the organisation i.e. it simply masks them.

One of the benefits of conducting a regular audit is that problems can be identified at an early opportunity before they affect the entire organisation and eliminate the need for crisis management.

The 'top 10' most common findings from an audit (Kotler et al., 2008) are illustrated in Table 5.3.

The findings or outcomes from undertaking a marketing audit need to be initially incorporated in a SWOT analysis (strengths, weaknesses, opportunities and threats), which forms part of the marketing planning process. It follows that the robustness of the audit will impact on the quality of the planning process.

ACTIVITY 5.1

For your own organisation, identify how often a marketing audit is carried out? Do you think changes should be made to the frequency and why? What barriers exist to this happening? How can these be addressed?

CHARACTERISTICS OF AN EFFECTIVE MARKETING AUDIT

Kotler and Keller (2006) identify that a marketing audit should be:

1. Comprehensive – Covers all main marketing activities

2. Systematic – Undertaken in an orderly structured manner

Table 5.3	Findings from the Marketing Audit
1. Knowledge	Lack of knowledge relating to customer behaviour and attitudes
2. Segmentation	Failure to segment the market effectively
3. Marketing planning	Lack of effective marketing planning procedures
4. Price	Price reductions implemented rather than increasing volumes
5. Evaluation	Lack of market-based procedures for evaluating products
6. Company strengths	Often misunderstood through a lack of research
7. Short-term view	Short-term position taken on the role of promotion
8. Marketing is advertising	The position is held that marketing is simply about sales and advertising rather than building long-term positions for an organisation
9. Organisational structures	The marketing structures in place are not effective in delivering customer-focused marketing activities in an effective manner
10. Lack of investment	Insufficient investment is made to support the marketing function

3. Independent – Carried out by someone who will not be biased in their assessment of the situation

4. Periodic – Undertaken at regular intervals not just when there is a perceived marketing problem in the organisation

Given the scale and depth of an effective audit, it is suggested that it is entrusted to a senior executive within the organisation. Often organisations will employ an internal audit team who will work with external auditors. The audit team whether composed of internal or external staff needs to be honest and rational in carrying out the audit if improvements to existing processes are to be made.

In conducting the audit, it is usually the senior management team who meet the auditors initially. Key members of staff will then be identified for interview as part of the process.

We have already noted not all organisations undertake an audit. This can be for a number of reasons including:

■ Cost; it can be expensive to undertake an audit, especially if external auditors are used. Staff may need to be taken away from their regular duties to support the audit and this represents another cost.

Table 5.4	Market Attractiveness Options
1. Ideal	Numerous opportunities identified but few threats
2. Speculative	High numbers of opportunities and threats identified
3. Mature	Low numbers of opportunities and threats identified
4. Troubled	Numerous threats identified but few opportunities

- Appointment of suitable auditors; selecting an auditor with the requisite skills may be difficult.

- Auditors will want to examine the areas identified above in great detail, and this is disruptive for staff that still need to carry out their day-to-day duties effectively.

Organisations are faced with an ever-changing marketing environment and need to have a comprehensive marketing information system in place to be able to effectively identify and track developments in the market to be able to take the necessary actions to improve their position. Trends can be categorised into opportunities or threats and an organisation will want to build on the identified opportunities while negating or minimising any threats.

Wilson and Gilligan (2005) suggest that an opportunity can be seen as any sector of the market in which the company would enjoy a competitive advantage. The opportunities can then be assessed according to their attractiveness and the company's probability of success in this area.

Similarly, threats can be categorised on the basis of the seriousness to the organisation and the probability of occurrence.

A company having assessed the opportunity and threats matrix will then establish a measure of the overall attractiveness of the market and four options exist, shown in Table 5.4.

However, the assessment above does not rank the overall attractiveness of the market in any way and the company must undertake a strengths-and-weakness analysis which ranks a range of factors and maps then against current performance factors, together with a ranking of their importance. In this way, a company can focus on the areas where it has a fundamental strength which is regarded as important.

It is the case that having conducted the above analysis a company will find there are too many potential opportunities to address.

The performance–importance matrix shown in Figure 5.2 will offer help.

Box 1 in Figure 5.2 consists of factors which have been identified as important but where the company is performing badly. Therefore, the organisation should focus on strengthening those factors, which are currently perceived as weak.

	Performance	
	Low	High
Importance High	1. Concentrate efforts	2. Maintain efforts
Low	3. Low priority	4. Possible over-investment

FIGURE 5.2

The Performance–Importance Matrix

Box 2 in Figure 5.2 consists of factors which the company has identified as performing well in areas which are important and it needs to maintain this position.

Box 3 in Figure 5.2 consists of factors which have low importance and where the performance is low.

Box 4 in Figure 5.2 consists of factors which have low importance and where the performance is high.

Having reviewed its position in the matrix, the company needs to focus on the areas of opportunity when the company has strengths, or where it can prove cost effective to acquire or develop new strengths.

QUESTIONS

1. Why should an organisation undertake a marketing audit?

2. Identify some of the practical constraints on performing effective marketing audits?

SUMMARY

This chapter has explored some of the practical issues of conducting a marketing audit. It recognises that not all companies undertake an audit and offers suggestions why this may be the case. Equally the important benefits of the audit to the planning process are identified i.e. where marketing opportunities and resources are assessed in relation to marketing objectives and the development of the plan to be implemented. It is an essential part of developing an overall marketing strategy and planning framework. Audits cover both the external (uncontrollable) elements as well as the internal (more controllable) elements. The audit needs to be conducted on a regular basis by a senior member of the company or by an external auditor who is objective. Areas for improvement can be identified and key areas can be prioritised and implemented.

BIBLIOGRAPHY

Kotler, P. and Keller, K.L. (2006) *Marketing Management*, 12th edition. Prentice Hall, Englewood Cliffs, NJ.

Kotler, P., Armstrong, G., Wong, V. and Saunders, J. (2008) *Principles of Marketing*, 5th edition. Financial Times/Prentice Hall, Harlow.

Wilson, R.M.S. and Gilligan, C. (2005) *Strategic Marketing Management: Planning, Implementation and Control*. Butterworth-Heinemann, Oxford.

Auditing the Market Environment

2.3   Appraise the process of auditing the marketing environment and make recommendations for the utilisation of various approaches in a range of different organisational contexts and sectors

2.3:

- past, current and future-oriented perspectives
- organising information for planning
- marketing audit structures, e.g. environment, strategy, organisation, systems, productivity and functions audits
- external and internal sources of information
- organisational and sectoral constraints
- using models and frameworks to facilitate understanding

INTRODUCTION

This chapter considers the structure of the marketing audit and how information can be gathered to fulfil the needs of the audit, taking account of both its external and internal dimensions. Key areas of the audit are identified within a framework for analysis that provides a basis for marketing planning relating to strategy development.

FRAMEWORK OF EXTERNAL FORCES

An organisation needs to be aware of the environment in which it operates and to do so effectively it has to consider a broad range of factors including:

- Political issues which may affect the company, not just in its home market, but any market it operates in. Political unrest and conflict, e.g. in unstable regimes with unsettled governments and terrorist attacks, may preclude opportunities for market entry.

- Economic drivers which may affect profitability. At the end of 2008, the Euro approached parity with the pound sterling, which had a significant impact on the costs of imports and exports into and out of the UK.

- Social and cultural considerations which affect the nature and demand for products bought. Family and household composition have been constantly changing in modern society away from their conventional structure, which has implications for a range of products and services.

- Technology is developing rapidly and this will affect both the pattern of consumer demand and the way in which products and services are produced and made available in the market. The Internet, for example, is changing purchasing behaviour and opening up new markets for businesses. Similarly it is used by organisations in offering their products in intermediary and distributor markets for business-to-business products and services.

- Environmental factors are a concern of many consumers as they become more aware of the impact that producing goods may have on the environment and the future of the planet (e.g. pollution from intensive agriculture and increased car usage on climate change). How will these motives stand up in difficult economic conditions when disposable income is reduced?

- Legislation may affect markets in terms of such measures as trade barriers and taxation. Further to this, it can affect individual consumer behaviour such as bans on smoking in public places or legislation to reduce risk in financial markets.

Collectively this is referred to as a PESTEL analysis. There are variations on the pneumonic, but this text will use PESTEL.

- Political
- Economic

- Social/cultural
- Technology
- Environment
- Legal

Organisations need to be active in understanding the importance of external forces. This became only too clear at the end of 2008 when a number of major high street names ceased trading with the loss of many thousands of jobs as a result of the severe economic conditions which confronted UK businesses. But were marketers and business analysts able to forecast this and the imminent 'credit crunch' and global recession?

In terms of the micro-environment, organisations need to be able to respond rapidly to the external changes identified and while this is usually focussed on expanding the business it can equally apply to situations where survival of the business is the main objective.

A critical aspect of planning for marketing is being able to identify changes in key forces in the environment both now and into the future, and this may also have its roots in understanding the past when similar circumstances previously existed. In the current difficult economic conditions, it may be possible to predict consumer and competitive behaviour from previous downturns in economic demand and use these insights to assist in planning marketing. For instance, it may be possible to anticipate competitive moves such as international trade barriers which may make it difficult to export, and possible shifts in consumption relating to necessity and luxury goods.

Organisations need to be able to collect and interpret information, and this is achieved through the process of environmental scanning, i.e. monitoring key information.

Beamish and Ashford (2008) suggest an organisation needs to be involved in two activities:

1. Environmental analysis
2. Environmental scanning

Environmental analysis is the process of analysing, assessing and interpreting the information collected through the scanning process.

Environmental scanning is the physical process of collecting the data from the external environment for analysis and interpretation. In particular, it focuses on the wider horizons of the environment that may affect the organisations in its markets in the future and can be summarised as:

1. Scanning the environment
2. Monitoring
3. Forecasting
4. Assessment

Drummond et al. (2008) identified five critical sources of external information which has been adapted in Table 6.1.

This information can be collected as a result of formal searches, information collection in general, informal searches or conditional viewing, i.e. not an organised search, but when the organisation is sensitive to information on certain topics.

ASSESSING THE INTERNAL POSITION

Understanding the internal environment is equally as important as the external environment for marketing planning and the key areas to be reviewed include:

Managerial functions

- Flexibility to change
- Level of innovation
- Ability to recruit and retain exceptional staff
- Responsiveness to change

Competitive factors

- Barriers to market entry
- Selling and distribution costs
- Market share

Table 6.1	Sources of External Information
Information area	**Category**
Market intelligence	<ul><li>Market potential; how big or profitable</li><li>Competitors and the industry: Competitor information and industry policy</li><li>Pricing strategies</li><li>Sales negotiations: Information on potential sales</li><li>Structural changes in the market e.g. mergers and acquisitions</li></ul>
Technical intelligence	<ul><li>Licensing and patents</li><li>New product processes and developing technology: Developing technology to be released into the market</li><li>Costs: Incurred by suppliers and competitors</li></ul>
Acquisition intelligence	<ul><li>Mergers, Joint ventures and acquisitions: Implications for the organization</li></ul>
Intelligence on broad issues	<ul><li>General conditions</li><li>Government actions and issues affecting the industry</li></ul>
Other intelligence	<ul><li>Suppliers and raw materials: Availability and continuity of supply</li><li>Resources available: People, equipment or premises</li></ul>

Financial factors

- Ability to exit or enter markets
- Access to capital
- Financial liquidity

Technical factors

- Economies of scale
- Value added to product
- Availability/access to technology

Each of these areas should be audited and the components of the audit are shown below.

ACTIVITY 6.1

For an organisation of your choice, identify the important external and internal areas of the audit for which information should be collected, and specify the sources of information that could be used to do this.

STRUCTURE OF A MARKETING AUDIT

An audit comprises six key components (Kotler and Keller, 2006):

1. Marketing environment audit
2. Marketing strategy audit
3. Marketing organisation audit
4. Marketing systems audit
5. Marketing productivity audit
6. Marketing functions audit

We will look at each of the components in turn, remembering that each individual organisation will develop an audit questionnaire which is bespoke.

1. Marketing environment audit

(a) The macro-environment
This part of the audit examines the PESTEL factors.

- Political/legal
    - What political or legal changes are being planned nationally or internationally which may impact on marketing activity?

- Are the levels of direct and indirect tax likely to remain stable?
- Will changes in legislation affect the way products are advertised?
- Economic
  - Major developments in economic conditions: how will sales be affected?
  - Is inflation increasing or decreasing?
  - How much disposable income will customers have to make purchases?
- Social/cultural
  - What do customers think of our products?
  - What lifestyle changes are taking place?
  - How are customer values changing?
- Technology
  - How is technology changing purchase habits?
  - What new technology is being developed or trialed?
  - Main technological trends in the industry.
- Environmental
  - Implications regarding 'green' issues.
  - Alternatives to current environmental procedures.

(b) Task environment

1. **Markets**
   - What trends are taking place, e.g. is the market consolidating through mergers or growing?
   - What are the key segments? How will they grow or contract?
   - What opportunities exist for market development?
   - Are any new markets expected to arise?

2. **Customers**
   - What are the needs and wants of our customers? Are we meeting them?
   - Do all the different customer segments purchase in the same way?

3. **Competitors**
   - Who are the main competitors and what are their objectives?
   - What changes are likely to take place in the competitive landscape?
   - Will there be a change in competitor ranking, i.e. will the strongest competitor maintain that position or will another new or existing competitor emerge?

4. **Distribution and dealers**
   - What are the main channels of distribution and how does the efficiency of each channel differ?
   - What new channels are being developed?

5. **Suppliers**

- Key trends emerging from suppliers and availability of supply
- Are new suppliers coming into the market or are existing suppliers leaving?

6. **Facilitators and marketing organisations**

- How effective are the organisation's advertising agencies performing?
- How are agencies utilising new technology?
- What are the trends for distribution and warehousing costs?

7. **Publics**

- Where are the opportunities and threats for the organisation?

2. Marketing strategy audit

This section of the audit considers:

- Marketing objectives
- Strategy

1. **Mission statement**

- Is the mission statement clearly stated in a marketing-orientated manner?
- How realistic is the mission statement and is it compatible with the organisation's corporate and marketing objectives?

2. **Marketing objectives and goals**

- Are the corporate goals clearly stated and do they guide the marketing objectives?
- Are the objectives consistent with the organisation's position and capabilities in the market?

3. **Strategy**

- Is the core strategy sound and will it achieve the objectives?
- How clearly is the strategy stated?
- Are there adequate controls to ensure effective monitoring?
- Are the positioning, segmentation and targeting strategies clear and appropriate?
- Are there sufficient resources to implement the plan?

3. Marketing organisation audit

Three aspects are evaluated:

1. **Formal structure**

- Is there a marketing director with the necessary authority for the company's marketing activities and customer satisfaction?

- How well is the marketing function structured and how is it structured?
- Are the current lines of authority adequate?

2. **Functional efficiency**

- How good is the communication between marketing and sales?
- Any additional training or controls needed?

3. **Interface efficiency**

- Are there any identifiable problems between marketing and other functions?

4. **Marketing systems audit**
   1. **Marketing information system**

- How effective is the marketing information system, does it provide accurate and timely information?
- Can all key managers access the system easily?
- Is the information clear?

   2. **Marketing planning system**

- Is the system well designed and effective?
- Is the system effective at forecasting sales and future trends?

   3. **Marketing control system**

- Do the systems offer the organisation a complete picture of efficiency and control?
- Are processes changed in the light of feedback or review?

   4. **New product development system (NPD)**

- Does the company have an effective NPD process to develop new ideas?
- Are new products effectively tested prior to market launch?
- Is the rate of new product development acceptable?

5. **Marketing productivity audit**
   1. **Profitability analysis**

- Are all the company's products analysed for profitability?
- Are there scenarios for entering new markets or withdrawing from non-profitable markets?

   2. **Cost-effective analysis**

- Do any of the marketing activities undertaken have excessive costs associated with them?
- Who has responsibility for monitoring costs?

6. Marketing function audit

1. Products and services

- What are the product line objectives?
- How appropriate are the objectives?
- Are there products which should be phased out?
- How does the product line compare with the competition?
- What products should be added or withdrawn?

2. Pricing objectives

- Are the pricing objectives, prices and strategies clear?
- Are the pricing objectives appropriate?
- Is price promotion used effectively?
- How responsive is the market to price changes?
- Are competitor prices monitored and reviewed?

3. Distribution

- Are the distribution strategies and objectives clear?
- How effective are the various channel members?
- Where does the balance of power lie with the channel?
- How can the effectiveness of the channel be improved?

4. Promotional mix

- Are the organisation's advertising objectives sound?
- Is the advertising effective?
- What research is conducted prior to advertising?
- How is the budget set?
- Is the Internet being used effectively?
- Are the various promotional mix budgets adequate?

5. Sales force

- Are the sales team's objectives clear?
- Is the team structured effectively?
- How effective is the sales team when compared to the competition?
- What is the rate of staff turnover?
- Where does staff move to?
- What do customers feel about the sales team?
- Are challenging targets set?

Adapted from Kotler and Keller (2006).

To give consistency to the finding of the audit and allow comparison with previous audits, organisations will often use a grading system based on Likert scale measures (e.g. ranking results on a 1–5 basis). This scale allows for a neutral position. Here, a '3' would be neutral and a '5' excellent, with '1' being unacceptable.

While many organisations operate without a formal or documented plan, Kotler et al. (2008) suggest that 'failing to plan means planning to fail'.

The process of formal planning allows a company to be clear on what it wants to achieve and how it intends to achieve those objectives. The argument for planning suggests and prepares for potential disruptions.

Companies usually set annual or long-range plans and the strategic plan gives direction to the marketing plan which contains the organisation's overall purpose for being in business along with its mission statement. This leads into SMART (specific, measurable, aspirational, realistic and time-bound) objectives being developed which can be evaluated. The audit (external and internal) then allows information to be collected on the company, competitors, the markets and the operating environment. The resulting strengths and weaknesses are evaluated and action plans developed in order for a decision to be made on the product portfolio to be made available to customers.

The audit is the start point for the marketing plan as it is concerned with building and sharing an agreed and objective understanding through a systematic process of data collection and analysis.

QUESTIONS

1. What are the key aspects of an internal audit?
2. What are the key aspects of an external audit?

SUMMARY

This chapter has considered the marketing audit structure covering the internal and external dimensions. It identifies the main areas of the audit and the key sources of information, and makes the link between the audit and the planning process.

BIBLIOGRAPHY

Beamish, K. and Ashford, R. (2008) *Marketing Planning*. Butterworth-Heinemann, Oxford.

Drummond, G., Ensor, J. and Ashford, R. (2008) *Strategic Marketing Planning and Control*, 3rd edition. Butterworth Heinemann, Oxford.

Kotler, P., Armstrong, G., Saunders, J. and Wong, V. (2008) *Principles of Marketing*, 5th edition. Financial Times/Prentice Hall, Harlow.

Kotler, P. and Keller, K.L. (2006) *Marketing Management*, 12th edition. Prentice-Hall, Englewood Cliffs, NJ.

The External Marketing Environment

2.4 Evaluate the external marketing environment through detailed analysis using marketing audit tools and techniques.

2.4:

- the evolving nature and extent of external environmental change
- marketing intelligence and environmental scanning
- macro- and micro-environmental analysis frameworks
- gauging the impacts of external forces on marketing planning
- identifying key external issues and assumptions
- external audit tools, e.g. PESTEL, Porter's Five Forces and strategic group mapping

INTRODUCTION

Having identified the practicalities and structure associated with the marketing audit, this chapter assesses the nature of the external market, identifies the key drivers of change and introduces some models and frameworks to aid the understanding of the external environment. From this platform marketing opportunities can then be identified and a competitive position for the organisation established to enhance its standing in the market.

FIGURE 7.1

*Levels of the Marketing
Environment*

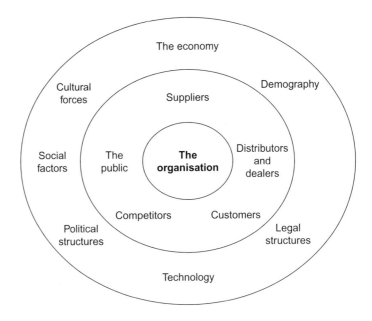

THE ENVIRONMENT AND MARKETING STRATEGY

Marketing strategy is concerned with matching the demands of the environment with the capabilities of the organisation. This can be problematic as the environment in which an organisation operates can be complex, diverse and continually changing. Figure 7.1 reflects the complexity of the situation.

Wilson and Gilligan (2005) suggest that the environment can be considered under two headings:

- The extent to which the environment affects strategy
- Understanding how environmental pressures can be related to organisational capabilities

However, we are warned not to just adopt a 'tick list' but develop a systematic approach.

We have briefly seen in the previous chapter that it is necessary for an organisation to scan and analyse the environment, and the various steps are outlined in Table 7.1.

Having completed the assessment, the firm's competitive position in the market can be established using strategic group analysis (see later) which highlights their relative degrees of market power. Finally the opportunities and threats facing the organisation can be established which will then form the basis for evaluating the organisation's strategic position.

Table 7.1	Scanning and Analysing the Environment
1. Scanning the environment	This is a general audit of the environment which identifies those factors which will influence the organisation. Trends and changes can be quickly acted upon
2. Monitoring	Monitoring changes and identifying opportunities and threats
3. Forecasting	Based on the available information change may need to be made
4. Assessment	An assessment of the potential impact on the business needs to be made

THE NATURE OF THE MARKETING ENVIRONMENT

The marketing environment consists of the macro- and micro-environments and the organisation (internal) environment. However in this chapter we will focus on the external influences on strategy, namely the macro- and micro-environments, represented by the two outside layers of the diagram.

The macro-environment consists of the broader elements and is often referred to as the 'non-controllable' elements.

It is the micro-environment which is nearest to the organisation and the one it can have more control over. We have already seen that the micro-environment consists of customers, competitors, suppliers, distributors and dealers as well as the public. Collectively these elements are often referred to as the 'controllable' elements, yet it is recognised that not all elements are controllable, although it is possible to influence them.

We will explore each of these two environments in more detail shortly, but it should be clear that the environment is a significant determinant of strategy and organisational performance.

Often organisations will adopt a proactive stance to change the nature of the market.

In 2008 the difficult conditions facing the financial markets brought about the merger of two large financial services organisations in the UK. Lloyds TSB and HBOS merged to form one of the largest banks in the UK. In normal trading circumstances, the merger would not have been allowed, as it would have been seen an anti-competitive because of the market share enjoyed by both organisations.

While the pace of change in the environment can usually be identified with some certainty, it was clear that the deterioration in the UK economy in 2008 caught many organisations off guard. Debate will continue as to whether this was a 'one-off' situation brought about by a unique set of circumstances which originated in the USA and therefore could not have been expected, or it was simply the scale of the situation which was not recognised. In either case, organisations will want to review their scanning processes for fitness of purpose to ensure that they are able to pick up signals of major changes in market conditions.

THE EVOLUTION OF ENVIRONMENTAL ANALYSIS

Wilson and Gilligan (2005) suggest that the:

> *'potential significance of environmental changes highlights the need for a certain type of organisational structure and culture which is then reflected in both a balanced portfolio of products and an adaptive management style supported by a well-developed intelligence and information monitoring system'*

Without this approach, organisations have an increased risk of missing key trends in the market.

It is not just trading organisations that need to stay alert to market changes. The FSA (Financial Services Authority) is charged with regulating banks and other financial services organisations in the UK. However, it was challenged over its monitoring of Northern Rock, a bank which had to be taken into public ownership because it was no longer able to access funds to pay its customers.

As the financial crisis deepened in 2008, the government was forced to take other organisations under public ownership to retain confidence in the financial markets.

Diffenbach (1983) suggests that there are three stages in the evolution of corporate environmental analysis:

1. Appreciation: looking beyond the short term and considering the wider PESTEL factors which constitute the business environment.

2. Analysis: finding reliable sources of data to develop trend analysis.

3. Application: real attempts are made to monitor the environment and assess the implications for change which are then translated into strategies and plans.

It has been suggested that there are three types of environmental monitoring processes:

1. Irregular systems where the process is focused on reacting to a crisis, i.e. fire fighting.

2. Periodic models where the irregular systems have been developed and are more systematic.

3. Continuous models where the periodic model has been developed and now looks towards the long term.

PESTEL ANALYSIS

The macro-environment looks at the broad range of factors that can affect an organisation.

Benefits of undertaking environmental analysis are wide, but include the following:

- Resource effectiveness. Changes to current resources can be planned for, increasing them to reflect a growing business, or reducing them when the market is contracting.

- Platform for change. Understanding and reacting to external changes enables the organisation to evolve and respond to market conditions.

- Planning efficiency. Understanding the organisation's strengths and weaknesses allows it to more effectively position itself in the market.

- External changes can be planned in a controlled way.

- Competitor positions and strategies can be understood and an effective respond developed.

The roles of the PESTEL (Table 7.2) analysis are the key factors which affect the industry generally and the organisation in particular. Using the model an organisation can develop a systematic approach to analysing the external environment.

Political

Organisations which operate within their own country are generally well aware of the political structures that are in operation. However, in the UK, there is also the Scottish Parliament and the Welsh Assembly which needs to be recognised. Equally the EU is increasingly becoming important in many activities. Organisations that operate in Europe need to recognise the different political structures and implications.

With the increasing number of global businesses, the political dimension is important for many organisations and generates opportunities and threats in equal measures.

Issues to be considered include:

- Taxation
- Trade protection
- Stability of political systems

Economic

Even if an organisation operates in the UK alone, it is not immune from the effects of economic conditions which are prevalent in other countries, both within and beyond Europe.

We have seen the effects on the UK economy of the housing market in the USA had in the UK. Icelandic banks went 'bust' leaving investors having to argue to get their money back.

Countries go through economic cycles and the Labour government was keen to avoid the 'bust and bust' approach adopted by the previous Conservative government.

While economies all across the globe go through the economic cycle illustrated in Figure 7.2, the difficulty is knowing the length of each stage of the cycle. Another key concern is the exchange rates of currencies. Many overseas organisations who had invested heavily in the UK were concerned at Britain's refusal to join the Euro, as this affected monetary exchange conditions and its influences on marketing such as price structures.

Issues to consider include:

- Spending patterns
- Consumer confidence
- Rates of exchange between different currencies
- Levels of direct and indirect taxation

Social/Cultural

The historic trend of better living standards has led to changes in the way we live, where we take out holidays and how we are educated. Equally the

FIGURE 7.2

The Economic Cycle

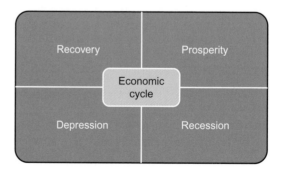

UK population is ageing and the number of people in employment and paying taxes is becoming a heavy burden. The increase in the number of people receiving a pension and the fact they are living longer is causing pressure on the pension funds of many organisations as well as the government.

Consider the way many of us buy music. Increasingly we download it from the Internet rather than buying a CD.

Social issues to consider include:

- Demographics such as:
  - Age, social class
- Religious beliefs, culture, ethics

Globalisation and the movement of people across continents have brought about some changes in cultural approaches (i.e. convergence), but nevertheless it is still an important consideration and covers:

- Language
- Religion
- Values
- Education
- Purchasing behaviour (finance, gambling, alcohol)

Organisations operating beyond their domestic market need to fully understand the markets through the process of research.

Technological

It can be argued that the pace of developing technology has never been faster. However, the role of technology and the benefits it delivers to the customer need to be clear. Often the effective use of technology can offer the organisation a competitive advantage.

Technology can affect both organisational and consumer behaviour changing the way things are made and the way things are bought respectively. It also affects behaviour in marketing channels: suppliers and intermediaries. For example, retailing has been revolutionised by online buying, but also through the way that manufacturers deal with their retailers in terms of stock ordering, delivery, payment, etc.

Environmental

There is growing awareness and concern for the environment. This has internal implications as well as political and legal considerations.

On the one hand, we can consider the environment from the perspective of climate change and the effects this is having on our weather systems.

Ultimately this may have a major influence on (for example) where we take our holidays and the resulting impact that may have on certain countries.

We can also consider it from the perspective of protecting the world's scare resources and the effective use of them.

Finally there is the pollution aspect to consider; this can be in terms of the products manufactured or the use of resources in the manufacturing process.

Legal

Often linked with the political dimension, but can range from international law covering merger and acquisitions to the concept of naming a product.

The amount and scope of legislation has been increasingly rapidly and covers areas such as honesty, decency and taste. Equally it is there to protect customers from the poor practices of some organisations as well as ensuring a certain standard of safety.

From an organisational perceptive, some legislation prevents it from operating in certain countries or buying or merging with another organisation because it may be seen as anti-competitive or simply the law does not allow ownership by overseas companies (Table 7.2).

COMPETITOR ANALYSIS

Understanding the organisations that compete in the same market is an essential requirement. The competition can attack using a number of approaches and by understanding them the appropriate response can be generated.

Competitor analysis is central to any marketing strategy and to ignore the competition is to assume the organisation operates in a vacuum, which it clearly does not.

In undertaking an analysis of the competition, key considerations will include:

- Marketing capabilities: how effective is their advertising and how much money is available for this activity?
- Levels of innovation: how innovative is the competition and how is innovation delivered?
- Management: how skilled is the management team?

A more strategic review would consider:

- Who exactly is the competition?
- What are the objectives?
- What strategies are being pursued and what success is being enjoyed?
- What are the main strengths and weakness that have been identified?
- How is the competition likely to behave and how will they respond to offensive moves?

Table 7.2	Summary PESTEL Analysis

PESTEL analysis

Political

- Taxation
- Stability of governments
- Protection of domestic markets from overseas companies
- Foreign trade agreements
- Environmental issues
- Monopoly controls

Economic

- Interest rates
- Inflation rates
- Economic cycle
- Unemployment
- Consumer confidence

Social

- Attitudes and values
- Culture
- Age profiles
- Social mobility
- Incomes
- Buying habits

Technology

- Rate of development of new technology
- Opening/closing of distribution channels

Environmental

- Green issues
- CSR
- Use of resources
- Pollution
- Climate change

Legal

- Restrictive practices
- Competition
- Safety
- Honesty

When we evaluate Porter's Five Forces model (Porter, 1980) we will see the importance of understanding the competition, but equally when we analyse and understand the competition we can build mechanisms to effectively compete against them, not just on price, but on a range of dimensions where a competitive advantage is held.

A competitor response profile will consider four dimensions as indicated in Table 7.3 and Figure 7.3.

Table 7.3	Competitor Response Profiles
Current strategy	How is the business currently competing and what success is being achieved?
Capabilities	What strengths and weakness do the competitors have and what resources are available to them?
Assumptions	What assumptions do the competitors hold about itself? How realistic are they and what is the basis of the assumptions?
Goals	What is it that drives the organisation and what are its goals?

FIGURE 7.3

Competitors' Likely Response Profiles

Having undertaken the analysis, the next step is to consider how the competition will respond to the broad changes and trends taking place in the market, and secondly how it will respond to actions taken by the competition. To answer the questions it is necessary to understand why the company is vulnerable, i.e. where its strengths and weaknesses lie.

Davidson (1987) identified a list of factors that made an organisation vulnerable and the list below offers a broad range of factors to be considered:

Finance
- Lack of cash
- Low margins
- High distribution costs

Resources
- Dated technology
- Staffing issues
- Old products

Markets
- Focus on one market sector
- Reliance on one/small number of customers

Kotler (2008) suggested that competitors will respond to change in different ways and grouped the range of change options into four categories:

Laid-back Competitor

The laid-back competitor responds only slowly to change and may justify this on the basis of its loyal customer base, simply not recognising the changes taking place. Alternatively while the changes taking place may be recognised it may be the case that the company does not have the resources to deal with the situation. In any event the rational for this approach needs to be understood.

Selective Competitor

Organisations may respond selectively to certain situations. It may never respond to price changes or sales promotions, but may react when a new product is introduced or an advertising campaign launched by a competitor.

Tiger Competition

The tiger competitor will respond quickly and aggressive to any organisation which attempts to move on to its 'turf'. A supermarket will respond very quickly to another supermarket that enters its market.

> In the credit squeeze of 2008, Tesco was coming under attack from the cheaper super-markets such as Aldi. Customers were moving to Aldi to take advantage of cheaper prices. Tesco responded by introducing a heavily discounted range of products to ensure customers remained loyal and were not tempted into competitor stores.

Stochastic Competition

Stochastic competitors do not show a predictable response and will respond in different ways to different situations making it very difficult to predict their behaviour and plan accordingly for it.

PORTER'S FIVE FORCES ANALYSIS

Porter (1980) suggested that an organisation should adopt a clear and mean-ingful basis for strategic thinking and his three generic strategies are:

- Cost leadership
- Differentiation
- Focus

In other words an organisation should understand its competitive stance and be clear what the organisation means to the customer. An organisation then needs to select the strategic approach which allows it to maximise its strengths recognising the competition. Porter then went on to suggest this could be done by taking into account five key factors (five forces).

The analysis that can be conducted is best completed at the SBU level and then aggregated up in order to provide a clear picture of the attractiveness of the industry to a particular organisation.

Understanding the 'forces' at work in a given segment of the market enables the organisation to decide whether to move into a particular segment.

The five forces are:

- Potential and new entrants and the threat of entry
- Substitute products
- Buyers and the power of buyers
- Suppliers and the power of suppliers
- Competitors and the nature of the competition

Figure 7.4 shows the five forces model. However, before an analysis of each area is undertaken, the following checklist should be used to asses the strategic implications of the competitive structure of the industry:

- What is the likely threat of a new entrant coming into the market and where is it likely to come from?
- What and where are the potential substitute products that may be used and what is the likely impact on the organisation and the industry?
- Who are the suppliers to the organisation and what power do they have over the organisation?
- Who are the buyers and what power do they hold over the organisation?
- Who are the present and future competitors and how strong is or will be the competition?

FIGURE 7.4

Five Forces Model
Source: Porter (1980)

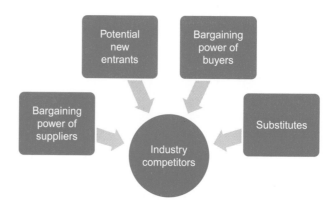

Taking each component in turn, Table 7.4 shows the five forces analysis of competition.

Table 7.4	Porters Five Forces Analysis of Competition

Potential entrants

What is it that is stopping a potential new entry from coming into the market? A key consideration will be the number of obstacles the organisation may encounter.
- The capital investment costs may be significant
- Economies of scale may be necessary to offset the entry costs and may not be achievable in the short term
- Access to distribution channels may be difficult and existing ones may need to be purchased or new ones developed
- Existing brands may have a loyal following and advertising costs to overcome this may be significant
- The existing competition may 'fight back' so making the market extremely competitive

Buyers

Buyers can be powerful in markets where:
- A small number of buyers control a large share of the market and can exert pressure on the suppliers
- There is backward vertical integration, i.e. the buyer purchases from the supplier removing the intermediary from the distribution channel
- The product lacks differentiation which lowers the barriers to alternative sources of supply

Substitutes

The threat of substitute products can arise in a number of ways
- The new product may replace the old product: MP3 players replacing CD players
- Consumer substitution, i.e. when one product is in competition with another, e.g. a weekend at Alton Towers theme park or a holiday in Spain
- Using Tesco Internet shopping rather than visiting the store

Suppliers

The power that suppliers hold is liable to be strong when:
- Few suppliers control a large share of the market
- The supplier has a strong brand that people associate with
- The cost of switching suppliers is high and this will act as a deterrent

Competitive rivalry

The intensity of the competition is affected by a range of factors:
- The size of the market, sometimes organisations, cannot grow any more without taking capacity out of the market. This has happened in the beer industry where brewers have bought other brewers just to take capacity out of the market
- Markets with a dominant player and many smaller players are likely to be less competitive
- Competitors of equal size will make the market more competitive
- Where the market suffers from a high proportion of fixed costs, competition may be high as a result of price discounting to maintain volumes
- Are there high barriers to leave the market?

STRATEGIC GROUP MAPPING

Having identified and analysed individual competitors in the market, it is then necessary to categorise the competition based on the strategies they are pursuing. The various competitors can be clustered together to see the competitive groups which have formed in the market as a whole.

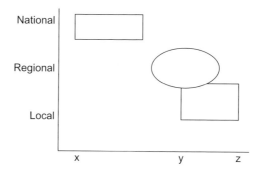

Figure 7.5 above represents three geographical distribution operations: local, regional and national for heating oil companies.

X: represents a group of companies which offer industrial and domestic fuels nationally

Y: represents a group of companies which offers industrial fuels only and on a regional basis

Z: represents a group of companies offering domestic fuel on a local basis.

Complexity can be built into the grouping and so we could map all the various production options, i.e. domestic and industrial fuel distributors, domestic only, industrial only against the geographical distribution options. This would allow a picture of the various strategic groups offering to be built and monitored.

A company who wants to enter the heating oil distribution market could use the strategic mapping exercise to identify where the main competition is and position itself accordingly. It should be noted that competition can still take place across the different strategic groups.

Similarly an organisation already in the market could use strategic mapping to develop competitive advantage for itself.

Various commentators have sought to identify the characteristics which can be used to define strategic groups and Table 7.5 highlights just some of the possible characteristics.

Table 7.5	Factors for Defining Strategic Groups	
Market share	Reputation
Product diversity	Distribution channels used
Market position	Geographic coverage
Market segments served	Product range
Branding	Size
Culture	Pricing

Strategic choice

Development strategies

Generic strategies

- Cost leadership
- Differentiation
- Focus

Alternative directions

- Do nothing
- Withdrawal
- Consolidation
- Market penetration
- Product development
- Market development
- Diversification

Alternative methods

- Internal development
- Acquisition
- Joint development

FIGURE 7.6

Strategic Choice
Source: Porter (1980)

COMPETITIVE ADVANTAGE

Competitive advantage (the process of identifying a fundamental and sustainable platform from which to compete with another or other organisations) is intrinsically linked with marketing strategy.

An organisation has a number of strategic choices available and we will explore Porter's approach in detail (Figure 7.6).

An organisation needs to have a competitive advantage which can be used to base its strategic activity on, which also supports the organisation's marketing programmes.

Porter suggests:

Cost Leadership:

This does not mean the organisation must offer the cheapest products, but that it develops and maintains a low-cost base. Economies of scale will be a

Table 7.6	Drivers of Cost Leadership

Infrastructure

The organisations' cost base is affected by a number of factors such as:
- Availability of skills. Many organisations located just outside major cities often find it difficult to recruit and retain staff because they prefer to work in the 'city'
- Government grants or funding (both domestically and overseas, e.g. European Loans) can affect location
- Technology such as the Internet is affecting the 'infrastructure' dimension by encouraging virtual locations and being able to establish a business in any location

Linkages and relationships

Here activities are linked together to produce cost savings.
- Airbus industries share production across specialist contractors which produces cost savings
- 'Just-in-time' supply is an effective way of reducing stockholding costs and the need for large warehouses

Economies of scale

Economies of scale are usually regarded as the single biggest influence on the cost structure of an organisation.
- Larger volumes of production generate cost savings and efficiencies (often citied as a reason for globalisation)
- Bulk or volume purchase also drives cost reduction

key feature. Overheads and other aspects of the business, such as marketing and purchasing, will be carefully monitored for cost efficiencies.

Drummond et al. (2008) suggest the basic drivers of cost leadership are:

- Infrastructure
- Linkages and relationships
- Economies of scale

Differentiation

An organisation will want to differentiate its products from the competition so that customers have a clear reason for making the purchase, rather than choosing a competitor's product.

Customers will select a product on the basis of the value the product adds: confidence, status, etc.

The basic drivers of differentiation are:

- Product augmentation
- Product perception
- Product performance

Table 7.7	Drivers of Differentiation

Product augmentation

The basic product offering is enhanced by adding value adding elements.
- The level of after-sales or technical service provided or the hours of staff availability.
- Easy access to finance

Product perception

For many people or groups of people, the perception of the product is more important than the product itself.
- The Ford Galaxy and the Seat Alhambra are two versions of the same car made by different manufactures.
- The brand Stella Artois is 'reassuring expensive', but may taste the same as other cheaper products.

Product performance

The actual performance of the product will also improve the product in the mind of the consumer and will be evaluated relative to the products offered by the competition
- Quality, durability and capability improve the performance of the product

Focus

Rather than concentrating on the mass market, the approach here is to 'focus' on a narrower approach. In other words, the organisation is concentrating its efforts on a smaller or niche segments. The organisation wants to develop specialist knowledge of the market.

The basic drivers of focus as illustrated in Table 7.8 are:

- Products and service specialism
- Geographic segmentation
- End-user focus

Table 7.8	Drivers of Focus

Products and service specialism

Highly differentiated, niche or premium products are developed
- A narrow or single product line could be developed, e.g. Steinway pianos

Geographic segmentation
- Production is based on the needs of the local market

End-user focus

Here the focus is on the specific needs of the end-user and then looking at a segment; it may be more effective to develop a profile

Organisational focus should be on one strategy, rather than trying to adopt different or mixing strategies. The effect of failing to adopt this approach is to become 'stuck in the middle' with the underlying principles of each approach being compromised.

Having identified the generic strategy, it needs to be developed into a specific competitive advantage which needs to be sustainable over the long term.

ACTIVITY 7.1

Consider a credit card company that wants to attract new customers. It offers all new customers the opportunity to transfer balances from other credit cards at 0% interest per annum, for six months.

What actions are available to the credit card company at the end of the interest-free period to stop customers moving to other competitors?

To be sustainable, Drummond et al. (2008) suggest the advantage must be:

- Relevant to the current and future needs of the market
- Defensible, i.e. barriers to copying which are:
  - Skills based
  - Asset based

English universities are seeking to end Scotland's competitive advantage in attracting overseas students.

Universities UK are calling for the Scottish Executive's Fresh Talent visa scheme to be extended to England, Wales and Northern Ireland.

The initiative, part of a drive to reverse population decline, allows overseas students a two-year visa extension if they study in Scotland.

There were more than 2,000 successful applicants in the scheme's first year.

The vice chancellor of the University of Bedfordshire, Prof. Les Ebdon, confirmed that there was envy, especially in the north of England.

Speaking on behalf of Universities UK, he said the scheme offered a 'significant competitive advantage' and should be extended to the rest of the UK.

'After all, international students bring in some £3bn a year to the UK economy, so it is very important business,' he said.

'As far as immigration rules are concerned we are supposed to be the one nation, we don't have devolved immigration rules.'

'It would be excellent to have the Fresh Talent scheme applied across the whole of the UK.'

'I know something like that will happen when the new immigration rules come into practice, but that could be a couple of years down the line.'

Boris Johnson, the Conservative higher education spokesman, described the situation as 'an anomaly'.

Unequal treatment

'Devolution was not intended to include immigration matters, and it is unjust to have an unequal visa treatment between Scotland and the rest of the country,' he said.

'I will be challenging Bill Rammell at the Universities UK annual conference to extend the Scottish visa regime to the rest of the United Kingdom.'

David Caldwell, the director of Universities Scotland, said it was understandable for the other UK universities to want to adopt the Fresh Talent initiative.

'It is not an uneven playing field, it is just a very good scheme,' he told BBC Scotland.

'The important thing is that it does not just benefit Scottish universities, it benefits Scotland.'

'Scotland needs to attract talent if we are going to have a thriving, growing, knowledge-based economy and these international students that come to Scotland bring the country great benefits.'

He said Scotland would not lose out if the rest of the UK adopted a similar scheme, as there were an 'enormous' number of overseas students who were interested in studying abroad.

'I hope for the benefit of our English counterparts that they will get something like it as well,' he added.

'Scotland and England can both be winners.'

The Home Office has already watered down the Scottish advantage by introducing visa extensions for overseas postgraduate students in England.

They will be allowed to remain in the UK for 12 months without a work permit after completing their studies.

Higher Education Minister Bill Rammell said 'significant changes' had been made.

Adapted from a BBC NEWS story:

http://news.bbc.co.uk/go/pr/fr/1/hi/scotland/5341092.stm

MARKETING OBJECTIVES, STRATEGIES AND PLANS

The marketing audit plays an important role in developing the marketing plan through a 'bottom-up' process which feeds it with key information about the organisation and the environment in which it operates.

Organisations need to ask themselves some important questions:

- Where is the business now?
- Where do we want it to be?
- How is it going to get there?
- How will we know when it is there?

QUESTIONS

1. When an organisation undertakes a competitor analysis, what are the three key considerations?

2. What do you understand by the term 'competitor response profile'?

3. What are the four key components in a competitor response profile?

4. In what ways can competitors respond to change?

5. What are the key components of Porter's Five Forces analysis?

6. Exactly what is the purpose of Porter's Five Forces analysis?

7. What do you understand by the term 'strategic group mapping'?

8. Why is it important for an organisation to develop a specific competitive position?

9. What are the three basic drivers of differentiation?

10. Porter's three generic strategies model suggests different positive positions an organisation can adopt, what are they?

11. A consequence of not adopting one of the positions is that the organisation becomes 'stuck in the middle'; what are the potential consequences of this?

SUMMARY

This chapter has looked specifically at the external (macro and micro) environments and has highlighted the importance of marketing intelligence and environmental scanning.

Organisations do not operate in isolation within the market and must appreciate and respond to the changes taking place in order to maintain or improve their competitive position. Some changes need to be spotted well in advance and organisations that use audit tools such as PESTEL, Porter's Five Forces and strategic group mapping will be in better position to respond to the external changes. Similarly understanding the nature and basis in which the competition acts allow robust challenges and positioning is to be established. Responses to changes made by the organisation's rivals can be identified and completion can take place beyond the basic concept of price and price changes.

BIBLIOGRAPHY

Diffenbach, J. (1983) Corporate Environmental Analysis in Large US Corporations. *Long Range Planning*, 16(3), 107–116.

Drummond, G., Ensor, E. and Ashford, R. (2008) *Strategic Marketing Planning and Control*, 3rd edition. Butterworth Heinemann, Oxford.

Wilson, M.S. and Gilligan, C. (2005) *Strategic Marketing Management*, 3rd edition. Butterworth Heinemann, Oxford.

The Internal Marketing Environment

2.5 Assess the internal marketing environment of an organisation through an audit process using a range of evaluation processes and approaches

2.6 Utilise the planning gap as a means to identifying and assessing key marketing planning requirements to fulfil the organisation's marketing strategy

2.7 Assess the issues and constraints arising from the marketing audit and consider the consequences for the organisation in order to develop its marketing plan

2.5:

- the evolving nature and extent of internal organisational change
- developing resource-based planning and strategy
- internal environmental analysis frameworks
- establishing the effects of organisational resources and capabilities on marketing planning
- identifying key internal issues and assumptions
- internal audit tools, e.g. product life cycle, portfolio models and the value chain

2.6:

- establishing objectives and the planning gap
- generating alternative strategic options

- filling the planning gap with new and existing strategies
- evaluating marketing opportunities and achieving competitive advantage

2.7:

- prioritising issues and executing SWOT analysis
- specifying marketing objectives, strategies and plans
- considering timescales for implementation

INTRODUCTION

The internal marketing environment is equally as important as the external environment and helps the organisation to identify how effective the internal resources and structures are in achieving the organisation's stated objectives.

In this chapter, we will be reviewing the frameworks which can be used for assessing the internal environment, examining the internal audit tools and considering the 'planning gap'.

INTERNAL CHANGE

We have already looked at the components of the internal marketing audit. Now we will examine the evolving nature of organisational change.

Drummond et al. (2008) suggest that to establish an organisation's current and potential capabilities, its assets and competencies should be established.

Organisational assets include:

- Financial, such as capital, liquidity and financial leverage
- Physical, which includes facilities and property
- Operational, such as plant and equipment
- People, i.e. employees and management
- Systems, such as marketing information systems

Competencies are the skills available to the organisation to enable it to use the assets identified above and are broken down into:

- *Strategic*: the management and strategic focus of the organisation

- *Functional*: the functional areas which manage the various activities (finance, marketing, human resources, etc) of the business

- *Operational*: responsible for the day-to-day operations of the organisation

FIGURE 8.1
*McKinsey Seven 'S'
Framework*
*Source: Peters and
Waterman (1982)*

- *Individual*: the individual skills and competencies which employees have

- *Team competencies*: how teams work together both within and across business functions

- *Corporate-level competencies*: skills which apply to the whole organisation

The internal marketing environment determines what the organisation is capable of delivering to its customers. Change to the internal environment is often necessary and the starting point for any change emanates from the strategy and structure in place.

The McKinsey Seven 'S' framework looks at the organisation from a different perspective identifying 'hard' and 'soft' shared values. Figure 8.1 shows the framework and reflects the concept that as each element is interlinked, a change in one area impacts on another area.

Strategy is the set of plans outlining how the organisation is going to achieve its objectives

Shared values are then guiding principles which lead the organisation into behaving in a particular way

Structure refers to how the organisation is structured functionally, i.e. who reports to whom

Skills are the capabilities that the organisation has as a whole

Systems are the processes and procedures which the organisation uses to meet customer needs

Style is the management approach collectively used

Staff are the people who constitute the organisation

INTERNAL AUDIT TOOLS

When undertaking an audit, a number of tools can be utilised to analyse the situation of an organisation internally and provide information on which decisions relating to marketing strategy can be taken. We will consider a number of these separately below.

PRODUCT LIFE CYCLE

Products are considered to have a finite life, which is referred to as the product life cycle (PLC) and the 'classic' view is shown in Figure 8.2. The PLC helps marketers to develop their marketing strategies as well as monitoring the progress of a product.

Marketers will want any newly launched product into the market to have as long a life as possible in order to generate an acceptable level of profit after the costs of development have been covered.

It is difficult to predict the life of the product and consequently the shape of the PLC can vary as modifications or changes are made to the product throughout its life.

A fad – a temporary period of unusually high sales volumes driven by consumer enthusiasm and immediate product or brand popularity will shorten the PLC.

Marketers will want to effectively manage each stage of the PLC and while the concept receives criticism it is undoubtedly a useful tool. As will be seen below, each stage of the product's life will be monitored, so that strategies can be developed. Pricing, product features, promotion (repositioning,

FIGURE 8.2

The PLC

rebranding) and distribution strategies will be reviewed at each stage and adjustments made as necessary.

Some organisations will find they have most of their products in the maturity stage and much time will be spent advertising the products, but with little thought being given to rebranding, repositioning or product modification. The changes made at this stage can be quite dramatic or subtle in delivery. For example, Mercedes Benz changed the shape of the headlights on its models to a 'teardrop' shape which attracted new sales. The PLC in Figure 8.2 shows sales and revenue plotted against time.

The key stages of the PLC are as follows:

1. Introduction

Generally, it takes time for a product to be accepted and sales can be slow at this stage. Depending on the investment, profit can be negative. However, the role of the marketer is to raise the level of sales with the target audience and widen distribution into the market to develop the product through to the next stage. Depending on the marketing objectives, a skimming or penetration pricing strategy can be adopted.

2. Growth

Sales start to rise quickly, possibly because there are now competitors in the market and more consumer awareness. The original product may be improved through the addition of new features to compete more effectively.

Profit is starting to rise at this stage and promotional activity needs to focus on brand building to encourage customers to purchase with less focus on price.

Brand building needs to be effective to encourage customers to buy from the organisation, rather than the competition, to build a strong position in the market and generating customer loyalty.

3. Maturity

Maturity tends to be the longest stage of the PLC, where sales now start to plateau and then fall. Profits come under pressure as the organisation focuses its marketing effort on countering competitive activity. However, the market becomes saturated and some of the weaker competitors will leave as profitability drops steeply. While many products at this stage remain unchanged, it is here that organisations develop enhanced versions of the product or launch new ones. Innovative use of the marketing mix can extend the maturity stage, i.e. prolong the life of the product, but eventually it will move into decline.

4. Decline

The decline stage can be a little unpredictable; sales can drop off dramatically, or follow a slow but steady downturn. The marketer has to decide on the most effective way of dealing with this by slowing down sales decline or by withdrawing marketing support and letting the product 'die', i.e. milking it.

Depending on the product, there is always the possibility of repositioning it in the customer's mind or to develop new markets or customers.

> Take for example Lucozade, which is the name for a range of energy and sports drinks. Originally a drink for people who were sick, designed to provide a source of energy, it was sold in glass bottle with an orange cellophane wrapper until 1983, when the slogan was changed from 'Lucozade aids recovery' to 'Lucozade replaces lost energy' along with a change in packaging. The glass bottle and wrapper was replaced with plastic. The rebranding was deemed a success as sales over a five-year period were reported as tripling. The brand still exists as a popular high-energy sports drink in a range of flavours, as well as the original.

The rapid development of technology increasingly forces manufacturers to consider letting the product die. We are currently seeing evidence of this in the 'demise' of video players and video tapes with CD players being replaced by MP3 players.

Organisations do need to understand that a failing product not only affects the organisation's profitability, but can diminish the brand in the consumer's mind if competitors are launching 'newer' or more advanced products.

ACTIVITY 8.1

For an organisation of your choice (this may be the one that you work for), analyse the portfolio of products that you produce in terms of the PLC stage that they currently 'fit' into. What are the implications for managing these products in future?

THE BCG MATRIX

Developed by the Boston Consulting Group (BCG) in the 1970s, it is generally regarded as an important model of marketing and strategic planning. The model helps organisations to identify potential opportunities and problems associated with a product. It does this by categorising the organisation's products into four.

The purpose of the BCG matrix is to help marketers develop their forward planning by suggesting strategies for the future development of the range: selectively invest in problem children; invest in and grow stars; maintain cash cows; and evaluate dogs removing them as necessary (MacDonald).

Many organisations, particularly those with large numbers of products, may find that they have a high percentage of dogs.

The BCG matrix (Figure 8.3) can operate at a number of levels including:

- Corporate
- Product
- SBU

It is based on the principle that cash, not profits, drives a product from one box to another within the matrix and helps an organisation to develop its growth strategies based on two-dimensional variables:

- Relative market share
- Market growth rate

Market share is measured against the product's nearest competitor, i.e. the degree of dominance the competitor enjoys, while market growth reflects the potential market opportunities and also indicates the organisation's likely cash needs.

The need which prompted this idea was, indeed, that of managing cash flow. It was reasoned that one of the main indicators of cash generation was relative market share and one which pointed to cash usage was that of market growth rate.

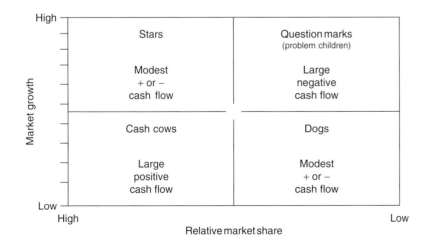

FIGURE 8.3

BCG Growth-Share Matrix

For each product, a circle can be plotted on the matrix to pictorially represent the relative value of sales in the category as well as likely cash flows.

The Quadrants of the BCG Matrix

Dog

A dog maintains a low market share in a low growth market and is likely to be cash neutral or consuming a modest amount of cash flow and resources.

A dog may have been a solid performer, but has subsequently declined in terms of performance. Given its low market share and lack of growth potential, the organisation will generally want to remove the product from the portfolio, unless the cash flow is strong in which case the product could be harvested.

Stars

A star occupies a high growth share in a high growth market. It generally requires a substantial investment to support expansion, but it is cash neutral and therefore regarded as a potential investment for the future.

Existing market share should be protected, or a larger share of new consumers should be sought.

Cash Cows

A cash cow maintains a high market share in a low growth market. It generates cash which can be used to support other products.

Market position or pricing should be maintained, or the profits used to invest in NPD.

Problem Child

Sometimes referred to as question marks, problem children will occupy a low market share of a high growth market. It consumes cash just to maintain its market share and requires cash to support product development.

Strategies for a problem child include divesting, harvesting or removing from the portfolio. Looking externally, another strategy is to buy a smaller product from competitor in order to build a large market share.

GENERAL ELECTRIC MATRIX

Another tool available to marketers is the General Electric (GE) matrix which, like the BCG matrix, uses a two-dimensional approach. Both models can be used as an aid to future planning or to evaluate an existing portfolio or the current level of investment in an SBU.

The GE matrix uses two dimensions: industry attractiveness and business strengths. In contrast to the BCG matrix, these dimensions are broken down into other factors which are rated and combined into an index of industry attractiveness. Business strength also uses an index which is then ranked strong, average or weak.

To use the GE matrix, an organisation would identify key factors which would make the market attractive to it. These factors would include the following.

Industry Attractiveness

- How large is the market now and in the future?
- What is the expected annual growth of the market?
- What are the expected profit margins?
- How easy is to enter the market?
- What is the competition?

Business Strengths

- Current market share
- Organisation's current rate of growth
- Ability to influence the market
- Available resources
- Current profit margins

Having compiled its strengths and ranked them strong, weak or medium, the organisation can then map them across industry attractiveness. This will then produce a position on the matrix.

The positioning on the matrix then offers three potential strategic options.

Where the organisation has identified strong or medium business strengths and the industry has been medium to high attractiveness (indicated x in Figure 8.4), it should invest for growth.

Having identified a market with low to medium attractiveness, linked with medium to weak business strengths (indicated xx on the matrix), then the consensus would be to withdraw from the market or harvest.

The remaining positions, i.e. weak strengths linked with medium to low industry attractiveness (xxx) on the matrix, should be managed selectively. Careful consideration is needed here to establish the most appropriate strategy.

THE VALUE CHAIN

The term 'value chain' was used by Michael Porter in *Competitive Advantage: Creating and Sustaining Superior Performance* (1985). The value chain analysis describes the activities the organisation performs and links them to the organisation's competitive position.

FIGURE 8.4

GE Matrix

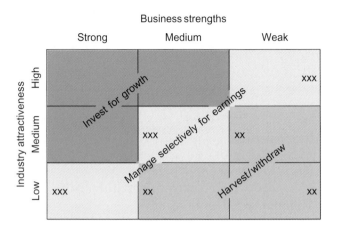

Value chain analysis describes the activities within and around an organisation, and relates them to an analysis of the competitive strength of the organisation. Therefore, it evaluates the value each particular activity adds to the organisation's products or services. This idea was built upon the insight that an organisation is more than a random compilation of machinery, equipment, people and money. Only if these things are arranged into systems and systematic activities, will it become possible to produce something for which customers are willing to pay a price. Porter argues that the ability to perform particular activities and to manage the linkages between these activities is a source of competitive advantage.

Porter distinguishes between primary activities and support activities. Primary activities are directly concerned with the creation or delivery of a product or service. They can be grouped into five main areas: inbound logistics, operations, outbound logistics, marketing and sales, and service. Each of these primary activities is linked to support activities which help to improve their effectiveness or efficiency. There are four main areas of support activities: procurement, technology development (including R&D), human resource management and infrastructure (systems for planning, finance, quality, information management, etc.).

The basic model of Porter's value chain is given in Figure 8.5

The term 'margin' implies that organisations realise a profit margin that depends on their ability to manage the linkages between all activities in the value chain. In other words, the organisation is able to deliver a product/service for which the customer is willing to pay more than the sum of the costs of all activities in the value chain.

These linkages are crucial for corporate success. The linkages are flows of information, goods and services, as well as systems and processes for adjusting activities.

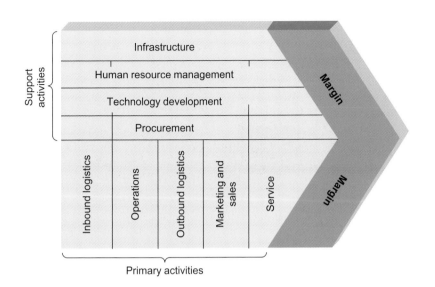

FIGURE 8.5

The Value Chain
Source: Porter (1985)

Only if the marketing and sales function delivers sales forecasts for the next period to all other departments in time and with reliable accuracy, will procurement be able to order the necessary material for the correct date. And only if procurement does a good job and forwards order information to inbound logistics, will operations be able to schedule production in a way that guarantees the delivery of products in a timely and effective manner – as pre-determined by marketing. To be successful, the linkages need to provide seamless cooperation and information flow between the value chain activities.

In most industries, it is unusual for a single company to perform all activities from product design, production of components and final assembly to delivery to the final user by itself. Often, organisations are elements of a value system or supply chain. Hence, value chain analysis should cover the whole value system in which the organisation operates (Figure 8.6).

Within the whole value system, there is only a certain value of profit margin available. This is the difference between the final price the customer pays and the sum of all costs incurred with production and delivery of the product/service (e.g. raw material and energy). It depends on the structure of the value system, how this margin spreads across the suppliers, producers, distributors, customers and other elements of the value system. Each member of the system will use its market position and negotiating power to get a higher proportion of this margin. Nevertheless, members of a value system can cooperate to improve their efficiency and to reduce their

FIGURE 8.6

*Relationships Between
Value Chains
Source: Porter (1985)*

costs in order to achieve a higher total margin to the benefit of all of them (e.g. by reducing stocks in a just-in-time system).

A typical value chain analysis can be performed in the following steps:

- Analysis of the organisation's value chain – which costs are related to every single activity

- Analysis of customers' value chains – how does our product fit into their value chain

- Identification of potential cost advantages in comparison with competitors

- Identification of potential value added for the customer – how can our product add value to the customer's value chain (e.g. lower costs or higher performance) – where does the customer see such potential

GAP ANALYSIS

The planning process requires an organisation to set objectives (where it wants to be) to be achieved in a specific time frame.

Organisations need to be able to monitor performance against objectives and while gap analysis should be conducted on a regular basis, it is an integral part of the marketing audit process.

Figure 8.7 shows the situation for an organisation that sets itself a £60 million target which was developed through the planning process from the corporate objectives.

However, sales are not as buoyant as originally forecast and there is a £30 million income gap in the plan (planning gap) identified. The organisation

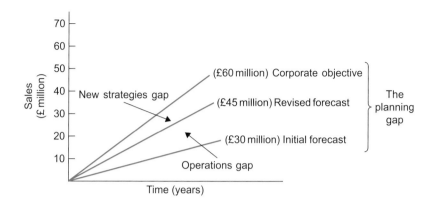

FIGURE 8.7
The Strategic Planning Gap

believes that it can reduce the gap by £15 million as result of introducing new strategies, which will now result in a £15 million gap

In reality, the marketing team would want to 'close the gap' and it can achieve this in a number of ways:

- Additional advertising
- Promotional pricing
- New distribution channels
- Product modification

Of course, it may have been that the planning process was flawed and incorrect assumptions were made, leading to inflated corporate targets being incorporated into the plan and this can have serious consequences.

Equally, the most effective planning systems cannot take into consideration the 'unthinkable' and that is what happened in '9/11' when the world's aircraft stopped flying and the airline market literally evaporated overnight. In such circumstances, organisations may find the only option is to look at a cost-leadership approach and eliminate as many costs as it possibly can out of the system.

Organisations do not just plan for sales but can include a range of objectives in their plans and Figure 8.8 illustrates some of the variables which can be measured.

GENERATING ALTERNATIVE STRATEGIC OPTIONS

In the previous chapter we identified options in terms of Porter's generic strategies, and we will now look at the alternative directions, in particular those derived from Ansoff's matrix. The matrix was developed in 1958 by Igor Ansoff and provides a linkage between the product and the market. Four strategic options are proposed for delivering a product to the market to ensure corporate goals are achieved.

FIGURE 8.8

Variance Analysis in the Planning Process
Source: Adapted from Luck and Ferrell (1979)

The four strategic options are:

- Market penetration
- Market development
- Product development
- Diversification

Market Penetration

Market penetration occurs when an organisation seeks to sell its existing products into an existing market. It will often adopt an aggressive marketing campaign offering price promotions or other incentives to encourage product take-up.

Market penetration can generate additional business quickly; however, there will come a time when the market becomes saturated and other strategies need to be pursued. A market penetration strategy has the least risk associated with it.

Market Development

Market development requires an organisation to offer an existing product to a new market. The new markets can include segments, distribution channels and overseas markets.

Product Development

Product development requires a new product to be offered to an existing market. Organisations through the PLC, for example, will be monitoring each product as it goes through the life cycle and will want to ensure it has a range of new products in development through its NPD process.

	Existing products	New products
Existing markets	**Market penetration** Ð Cross selling Ð Wins from competitors Ð Lower price Ð Advertise more	**Product development** Ð Modified or new products to existing markets, e.g. electronic banking services
New markets	**Market development** Ð Identifying new markets for existing products, e.g. joint ventures, geographic expansion	**Diversification** Ð Start or buy business outside current products and markets, e.g. portals, third party distribution channels

FIGURE 8.9

Ansoff's Product Market Matrix

Diversification

This strategy requires not only a new product but also a new market and consequently this approach carries with it the highest level of risk.

Diversification can be 'related', i.e. have some connection with existing activities, or 'unrelated', where there is no connection with any existing activities. Clearly, diversification is moving an organisation into new territory, and as can be seen in Figure 8.9, it can involve the purchase of a new business. Of course with risk comes reward and diversification may be an essential strategy for some organisations.

Organisations should not pursue one approach at the expense of others. It is usually necessary to be pursuing two or more strategies at the same time if organisational objectives are to be achieved.

ACTIVITY 8.2

For your own organisation, or one you are familiar with, identify and explain a market penetration strategy, and a market development strategy.

Dell's diversification pays off

Dell, the world's second biggest PC-maker, has posted a 21% rise in third-quarter profits.

Texas-based Dell's financial results were broadly in line with IT analysts' expectations.

Dell said it made net profits of $677 m in the three months to end-September.

Improved sales of servers and data storage systems for the commercial sector lifted revenue to $10.6 bn from $9.14 bn year-earlier, up 16%.

Smart strategy

Dell's latest financial results showed the benefits of its efforts to diversify its product range.

It has expanded into printers, data storage systems and cash registers in recent years.

In September, it announced plans to take the process a step further by launching its own digital music players and TVs.

Dell slashed PC prices in August in hopes of stimulating sales.

PC sales have remained sluggish worldwide for the past three years.

Dell specialises in selling inexpensive PCs by shipping direct to consumers, cutting out the retailer.

Price cutting by PC makers has pushed prices down 40% since 1997, according to analysts at investment bank Merrill Lynch.

Dell's third quarter results were released ahead of schedule, coming shortly before the market closed. Its shares bounced upwards before dipping 3 cents to $35.64.

Source: Adapted from a BBC NEWS:
http://www.news.bbc.co.uk/go/pr/fr/-/1/hi/business/3269299.stm
Published: 2003/11/13 21:47:47 GMT
© BBC MMIX

SWOT ANALYSIS

SWOT analysis is the commonest structure for bringing together the strengths, weaknesses, opportunities and threats which have been identified as part of the audit.

Environmental factors relating to the internal and external position of an organisation need to be captured at all the various levels (typically the SBU) and categorised into strengths, weaknesses, opportunities or threats.

Having identified and categorised the various elements, an organisation will want to convert weaknesses and threats into strengths and opportunities (Figure 8.10).

Strengths and weaknesses are internally focused elements (but can be reflected externally) and opportunities and threats are externally focused.

A SWOT analysis will produce a wide range of information which the organisation needs to analyse and decide on a programme of actions which, the needs to be developed into a performance-importance matrix.

Opportunities need to be prioritised in terms of importance and threats similarly need to be ranked in terms of the seriousness of the threat.

FIGURE 8.10

SWOT Analysis

Table 8.1 offers some examples of the contents of a SWOT analysis.

Table 8.1	Contents of a SWOT Analysis
Strengths	**Weaknesses**
■ Strong brand awareness	■ High staff turnover
■ Experienced management team	■ Lack of investment funding
■ Innovative culture	■ Poor channel relationships
■ New technology	■ Excess product capacity
Opportunities	**Threats**
■ New distribution channels available	■ New players entering market
■ Dealer loyalty becoming important	■ Low margins in market
■ Demand for new products	■ Cost of new technology high
■ Internet/e-commerce initiatives	■ Competitive market

It can be the case that factors identified as a strength can also be a weakness. Take the example of a brand. An organisation may have a very strong brand with consumers, but equally the brand in other sectors of the market may be viewed as large and uncaring.

SWOT analysis underpins decisions relating to the selection of strategies based on evaluation of various criteria, and these can be related to the target market segments that we can choose to focus upon with particular market offers. The link of this process into strategy and segmentation – targeting and positioning in particular – is made in the following chapter.

QUESTIONS

1. What is meant by the term 'internal environment'?
2. Draw the GE matrix and explain the various components.

3. Explain the concept of the PLC. Of what value is it to marketers?
4. What is the BCG matrix? Explain how it is developed and used in strategic marketing decisions.
5. What do you understand by the term 'star'? How should they be managed?
6. What is the role of the GE matrix?
7. What do you understand by Porter's value chain?
8. What is the purpose of 'gap analysis'?

SUMMARY

The internal marketing environment is equally as important as the external environment and helps the organisation to identify how effective the internal resources and structures are in achieving the organisation's stated objectives.

This chapter has reviewed a number of key frameworks which marketers can use to assess the internal environment, examining the internal audit tools and considering the 'planning gap'. Models like the BCG matrix help an organisation to ensure that it is maximising its cash flow through the careful management of the portfolio. The advantages and disadvantages of the model and other models have been discussed. However, the financial turmoil at the start of 2009 demonstrated the importance of retaining cash in the business.

Porter's value chain demonstrates the need for value to be added to a product, and the cost of the value-adding process should not exceed the additional income which can be generated. The concept of 'gap analysis' is examined and its importance to the organisation in ensuring that when, for example, sales are lower than planned at a given point, corrective and timely action can be taken. Ways of filling this gap are identified using combinations of products and markets. SWOT is then introduced as a basis for facilitating these decisions of selecting marketing strategies.

BIBLIOGRAPHY

Drummond, G., Ensor, E. and Ashford, R. (2008) *Strategic Marketing Planning and Control*, 3rd edition. Butterworth Heinemann, Oxford.

Luck, D.J. and Ferrell, O.C. (1979) *Marketing Strategy and Plans*. Prentice-Hall, Englewood Cliffs, NJ.

Peter, T. and Waterman, R. (1982) *In Search of Excellence: Lessons from American's Best-Run Companies*. Warner Books, NY.

Porter, M.E. (1985) *Competitive Advantage: Creating and Sustaining Superior Performance*. Free Press, New York.

Senior Examiner's Comments – Section Two

On completion of Section 2, students should have a detailed knowledge and understanding of:

- The practical issues associated with undertaking a marketing audit.

- The structure and content of a marketing audit.

- The sources of information available for inclusion in the audit process.

- The dimensions of the internal marketing audit and the identification of marketing opportunities.

- The constituent components of the internal marketing environment.

- The process of analysing audit information to generate strategic options.

An important factor in student success is the ability of applying the marketing audit process in different types of organisation and understanding the particular constraints that they may be faced with in each case. It is especially important that candidates are prepared for the information gathering process that is involved in auditing the internal and external marketing environments, and how this can be analysed to form the foundation for marketing strategies and tactics. Being objective in analysis of audit material is critical to the formulation of effective strategies. Similarly, effective implementation of marketing plans needs to take account of the constraints on undertaking an audit in different situations and the timeliness and cost trade-off of data availability in these scenarios.

Finally, students not only need a thorough understanding of audit tools and the contribution that each can make to analysis, but also be able to evaluate their use in the audit process. This also applies when bringing together information on both the internal and external situations of an organisation to provide a framework for generating strategies that provide the focus of a marketing plan.

Creating Marketing Strategies Through Segmentation, Targeting and Positioning

CHAPTER 9

The Role of Marketing Strategies and Market Segmentation

3.1 Critically evaluate the role of marketing strategies and demonstrate how they can be used to develop competitive advantage, market share and growth

3.2 Assess the importance of market segmentation as a basis of selecting markets to achieve the organisation's business and marketing objectives via customer satisfaction

3.3 Critically evaluate the different segmentation approaches available to organisations in different organisational contexts and sectors and make recommendations for their use

3.1:

- marketing strategies for meeting marketing objectives through satisfying customer requirements
- marketing strategies as product 'offers' providing benefits to customer segments
- identifying customers and offers for future development
- defining local, national, international and global markets and their parameters
- principle of market segmentation, targeting and positioning
- benefits and costs of market segmentation
- conditions for successful segmentation

3.2:

- defining local, national, international and global markets and their parameters

- principle of market segmentation, targeting and positioning
- benefits and costs of market segmentation
- conditions for successful segmentation

3.3:

- segmentation variables for business markets
- segmentation variables for consumer markets
- profiling segments and defining customer types
- critical evaluation of segmentation techniques
- contemporary methods of segmentation such as relationship-based approaches and online behaviours

INTRODUCTION

The third section of the syllabus is focussed on segmentation, targeting and positioning (STP). Students will need to be able to critically evaluate strategic options within this stage of the marketing planning process and propose outcomes that relate to determining competitive strategy.

Of particular importance is the recognition that strategies need to be assessed in terms of their future contribution to the organisation's specific contextual objectives. In addition, students need to become familiar with the notion that both internal and external factors should contribute to any appraisal of the attractiveness of the value of alternative market segments.

MARKETING STRATEGY

Dibb et al. (2006) define marketing strategy as 'a strategy indicating the opportunities to pursue, specific targets, and the types of competitive advantages that are to be developed'.

A strategy requires clear objectives and focus aligned with the organisation's corporate goals.

Marketing strategy addresses three separate aspects of marketing planning:

1. Customers
2. Competition
3. Internal issues

A staged approach to marketing strategy development suggests the sequence of:

- Identifying mission, vision and corporate strategy of the organisation
- Undertaking opportunities, capabilities and resources analysis
- Scanning the environment for information relating to customer and competitor analysis
- Segmentation, targeting and positioning

Looking at the sequence above, we have already addressed some of the issues so in summary:

- A marketing opportunity is a set of circumstances and timings that allows an organisation to take actions towards *reaching* a target market.

How attractive the market is to an organisation will be determined by a number of forces and factors which will be determined by a strategic analysis of:

- external environment through environmental scanning;
- internal analysis identifying the relative competencies and capabilities of the organisation;
- the strengths, weakness, opportunities and threats faced now and in the future;
- customer analysis to identify their needs and wants, so the organisation can understand them and respond to changing requirements.

ACTIVITY 9.1

For your own organisation or one you know well, identify what you believe to be the marketing opportunities available to it in the short, medium and long term.

The next step is to formulate a strategy based on the analysis and this will include establishing STP. This will be discussed in detail below; but by way of introduction from a strategic perspective, the following overview is provided.

Segmentation is the process of breaking down a large market into small manageable sub-divisions where the organisation can build up a detailed picture of the segment and offer it a specific marketing offering. Customers respond well to marketing approaches, which they perceive addresses their needs. It could be argued that organisations that do not fully understand the needs of their customers will find it difficult to develop an effective marketing strategy.

Organisations having segmented a market will then pursue *targeting* one or more segments through marketing programmes. This is done on a priority basis, often based on the simple concept of which segment is going to be more profitable. For some not-for-profit sectors, priority can be on which sector(s) has the greatest needs or fulfil the most non-profit objectives. Effective targeting requires a number of decisions to be made on the best use of the marketing mix and whether the same mix needs to be used across each target segment.

An organisation then needs a clear *positioning* in the mind of the consumer and to develop a distinctive perceived location in the market relative to the competition, based on matching the product to the identified needs and wants of the customers.

MARKET SEGMENTATION

Organisations do not have finite resources and need to use the resources they do have in an effective manner. After all, a poorly targeted marketing programme not only affects sales but takes away financial resources which could have better used, not just on other marketing programmes but on other divisions of the organisation.

We will be exploring the concept that, by identifying people or organisations that have similar needs and wants, marketers can be more effective by focussing resources and marketing programmes on those segments which have been identified as being more likely to make purchases.

CACI makes the point: 'People in similar areas have the same needs and lifestyles'.

Before we define what we mean by 'segmentation', we need to understand the term 'market' and the context in which it will be used.

Dibb et al. (2006) suggest that a market is 'an aggregate of people who, as individuals, or within organisations, have a need for a certain products and the ability, willingness and authority to purchase such products'.

This is an important concept because we can divide the market into business (B2B) and consumer markets (B2C) that will have different requirements, which can be satisfied through effective segmentation.

The concept of segmentation was developed by Smith (1956) and has been defined by Dibb et al. (2006) as:

'The process of grouping customers in markets with some heterogeneity into smaller, more similar or homogeneous segments.'

They go on to define a market segment as:

> 'A group of individuals or organisations sharing one or more similar characteristics that cause them to have relatively similar product needs and buying characteristics.'

The concept of segmentation applies to both consumer and business (organisational) markets, and we will explore each separately. Although they enjoy similarities, there is the added complication in business markets that buying decisions, while being made by individuals are usually made by the 'buying centre' or decision-making unit (DMU) where responsibility for different aspects of the process are given to specific people or functions.

The stages of the STP process can be identified as follows.

Situational Analysis

- Identify and organisation's current position, capabilities, objectives and constraints

Market Segmentation

- Identify the segmentation variables and segment the market
- Develop profiles for each segment

Targeting

- Evaluate the potential and attractiveness of each segment
- Select the target market segment(s)

Product Positioning

- Identify the position within each target segment
- Select and develop the appropriate positioning concepts

Marketing Mix

- Develop the marketing mix strategy

BENEFITS OF SEGMENTATION

Organisations may have different objectives depending on the market they are operating in. Charities will have different objectives from a private company.

However, no organisation generally has the resources or appeal to be in every market.

Choices have to be made about which market or segment to operate in and equally where not to be.

Doyle (1994) offered organisations a number of benefits which accrue from segmenting a market and they are summarised below.

- A distinct marketing mix can be produced for each segment which gives it a specific solution for their requirements.

- Focussed communications through specific channels can be used, e.g., trade rather than national press.

- Customer retention – It is far more expense to recruit new customers than to retain existing ones, so by developing a specialism and understanding in specific segments, customers are more likely to stay with the organisation.

- Market leadership – Brand leaders in segments are generally very profitable.

- Profits – It is the desire of most organisations to make a surplus over costs which can be reinvested in the business.

- Segmentation also allows an organisation to differentiate itself and its products from the competition and therefore position itself clearly in the customer's mind through a different marketing approach for each segment.

SEGMENTING BUSINESS MARKETS

Business markets have:

- Macro- and micro-segments

Macro-segments are subgroups which share common characteristics with the whole market.

Macro-segments are based around different buying characteristics.

Macro-segmentation

Macro-segments can be divided into organisational characteristics and product applications characteristics (Tables 9.1 and 9.2).

Local authorities in the UK have generally in the past made their own individual purchasing decisions. There is a growing trend in the sector to join with another local authority to combine not only purchasing power but expertise.

Table 9.1	Macro-segmentation of B2B Markets

Organisational

Size of an organisation

- The size of an organisation will often affect the purchasing process. Larger organisations will often have a formal purchasing procedure in place, not only to provide consistency but also to ensure the process is transparent to suppliers and other parties. The 'risk' (financial and reputational) associated with the purchase is another consideration.

Location

- Often organisations specialise in local or specific geographical areas. This is evident in technology or retail parks.
- Banks often locate their overseas offices in key financial locations across the globe.
- Increasingly, some organisations only want to serve 'local' areas because of specialisation or environmental issues.

Usage

- The level of product 'usage' is another way to segment the market. An organisation may want minimum purchase levels to make it effective to conduct business or it may introduce different price points depending on the level of purchase.

Product

Standard customer groupings

- A standard industrial classification (SIC) code in the UK; all businesses are defined by SIC codes which identify legal status and industry sectors which can then be broken down into more detailed segments.

Specific application

- Defining a specific product application and grouping the customers around that.

Table 9.2	SIC Codes as Macrosegments

Example SIC codes

The agricultural sector is quite diverse and only a very specific segment may need to be targeted. SIC 01000 covers farming generally, but SIC 01330 covers fruit, nuts, beverage and spice crops, so quite specific.

01000
Agriculture, hunting and related service activities.

01100
Growing of crops, market gardening and horticulture.

01110
Growing of cereals and other crops not elsewhere classified.

01120
Growing of vegetables, horticultural specialities and nursery products.

01130
Growing of fruit, nuts, beverage and spice crops.

Within the broader macrosegmentation approach, it is possible to identify another subgroup or microsegment. However, this can be quite specific and an organisation would generally have to explore a wide range of information sources to obtain the level of detail necessary.

Micro-segmentation

This approach relates to factors associated with the buying process in organisations, such as the DMU, the DMP, purchasing strategy and relationships (Table 9.3).

SEGMENTING CONSUMER MARKETS

It is generally the case that consumer markets are larger than business markets and can be subjective and variable.

Figure 9.1 shows a range of segmentation variables for the consumer market.

Geographic Segmentation

This is a popular form of segmentation and can take into consideration markets beyond domestic boundaries. At its broadest, it can identify continents, regions, countries, which can be subdivided into cities, towns and villages.

Organisations which operate on a global or international basis often divide the operation into global regions to reflect the culture of a particular region.

Geographical segmentation is often used in conjunction with other forms of segmentation. Consider an UK-based company who operates internationally and are keen to standardise their products to take advantage of economies of scale. If it only segmented on the basis of geography, it

Table 9.3	Micro-segmentation of B2B Markets
Structure of DMU	
▪ The roles and responsibilities of the DMU.	
Purchase decision process	
▪ Is a competitive tender needed?	
Purchasing strategy	
▪ Does the organisation have one supplier for each product or multiple suppliers?	
Buyer–seller relationships	
▪ Collaborative or adversarial approach?	

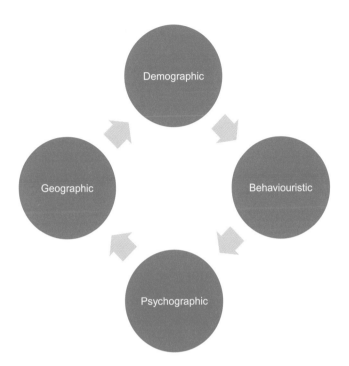

FIGURE 9.1

Approaches to Segmenting Consumer Markets

would be unable to compete effectively with the local competition who are likely to be adopting a more robust form of segmentation. The additional segmentation approaches to be adopted will depend on the organisation's marketing strategy.

On a more local basis, if an organisation wants to expand its business, it may want to establish a presence in major towns or cities where the size of the population within the catchment area is believed to be sufficient to operate a viable business.

Similarly organisation may want to expand on a defined regional basis so that it can effectively control the business as a result of its local nature.

VISA THE WORLD LARGEST PAYMENT PROCESSOR

Visa Inc. is headquartered in San Francisco. The company has five operating regions: Asia-Pacific; Canada; Central and Eastern Europe, Middle East and Africa; Latin America and Caribbean; and USA.

Visa Europe is a separate entity that is an exclusive licensee of Visa Inc.'s trademarks and technology in the European region.

Source: Visa.com

Demographic Segmentation

Demographic segmentation takes into account a broad range of characteristics, which the marketer must clearly define. It provides a broad picture of the customer enabling a finely targeted approach to be developed.

Car insurance companies can target the over 50s and offer cheaper insurance because the sector is generally considered to be safer. Similarly, other car insurance providers may actively avoid the under-21 age group because they are more likely to have an accident.

Some products are clearly tailored to the needs of the segment. Club 18–30 holidays are designed to appeal to that age group.

Clothing retailers aim at particular market segments, with some owning different retail brands for different target customer groups.

ACTIVITY 9.2

Consider the following high-street stores: Next, Marks & Spencer and Debenhams. What segments of the market do they appeal to?

Family life cycle segmentation assumes consumers will live their lives through a range of alternative scenarios and is shown in Figure 9.2. The cycle will continue until old age and retirement.

Banks offer a range of accounts to different age groups. Typically, young children are offered a savings account only. At around 12 years of age, the bank will offer an account which has immediate access through a debit card. At 18, for those going to University, a student account can be opened with greater financial flexibility reflecting the individual's situation.

The customer may then marry and want a home loan, followed by a saving account for their children. Understanding the family cycle and the customer's position within it, allows for a long-term relationship with the provider that offers different services products throughout the life cycle.

Geodemographic Segmentation

Geodemographic segmentation combines demographic and geographic variables. It is an analysis of where people live and combines lifestyle data with location (postcode data).

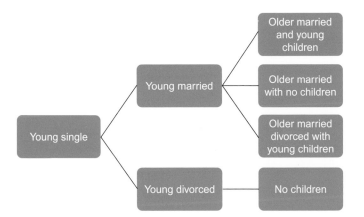

FIGURE 9.2

Family Life Cycle Groups

ACORN

ACORN is a geodemographic tool used to identify and understand the UK population and the demand for products and services. Businesses use this information to improve their understanding of customers, target markets and determine where to locate operations.

Informed decisions can be made on where direct marketing and advertising campaigns will be most effective; where branches should be opened or closed; or where sites are located, including retail outlets, leisure facilities and public services.

ACORN categorises all *1.9 million UK postcodes*, which have been described using over *125 demographic statistics* within England, Scotland, Wales and Northern Ireland, and **287** *lifestyle variables*, making it the most powerful discriminator, giving a clearer understanding of clients and prospects.

People in similar areas are assumed to have similar demographics, lifestyles and buying behaviour (Table 9.4).

Psychographic Segmentation

The previous segmentation strategies discussed have been reasonably straightforward to define and measure. Psychographic segmentation is more problematic because of its nature. It is sometimes referred to as lifestyle segmentation and perhaps this gives some clue as to its complexity.

Psychographic segmentation looks at variables such as beliefs, opinions, motives and aspirations, which collectively make 'lifestyle'. Psychographic data can be used on its own or in conjunction with other variables.

Such data is being increasingly used as it can be a better identifier of product usage. For example, some people would prefer to buy an organic wine, others a 'value for money' brand or supermarket special offer while for some nothing less than vintage Bordeaux would be acceptable.

Table 9.4	ACORN Classification (CACI)	
Category	**Group**	**Type**
Wealthy achievers	Wealthy executives	01 – Affluent mature professionals, large houses 02 – Affluent working families with mortgages 03 – Villages with wealthy commuters 04 – Well-off managers, larger houses
	Affluent greys	05 – Older affluent professionals 06 – Farming communities 07 – Old people, detached houses 08 – Mature couples, smaller detached houses
	Flourishing families	09 – Larger families, prosperous suburbs 10 – Well-off working families with mortgages 11 – Well-off managers, detached houses 12 – Large families and houses in rural areas
Urban prosperity	Prosperous professionals	13 – Well-off professionals, larger houses and converted flats 14 – Older professionals in detached houses and apartments
	educated urbanites	15 – Affluent urban professionals, flats 16 – Prosperous young professionals, flats 17 – Young educated workers, flats 18 – Multi-ethnic young, converted flats 19 – Suburban privately renting professionals
	Aspiring singles	20 – Student flats and cosmopolitan sharers 21 – Singles and sharers, multi-ethnic areas 22 – Low-income singles, small-rented flats 23 – Student terraces
Comfortably off	Starting out	24 – Young couples, flats and terraces 25 – White-collar singles/sharers, terraces
	Secure families	26 – Younger white-collar couples with mortgages 27 – Middle income, home-owning areas 28 – Working families with mortgages 29 – Mature families in suburban semis 30 – Established home-owning workers 31 – Home-owning Asian family areas
	Settled suburbia	32 – Retired home owners 33 – Middle income, older couples 34 – Lower income people, semis
	Prudent pensioners	35 – Elderly singles, purpose built flats 36 – Older people, flats
Moderate means	Asian communities	37 – Crowded Asian terraces 38 – Low-income Asian families
	Post industrial families	39 – Skilled older family terraces 40 – Young family workers
	Blue-collar roots	41 – Skilled workers, semis and terraces 42 – Home owning, terraces 43 – Older rented terraces

(*Continued*)

Table 9.4	(Continued)	
Category	**Group**	**Type**
Hard pressed	Struggling families	44 – Low-income larger families, semis 45 – Older people, low income, small semis 46 – Low income, routine jobs, unemployment 47 – Low rise terraced estates of poorly-off workers 48 – Low incomes, high unemployment, single parents 49 – Large families, many children, poorly educated
	Burdened singles	50 – Council flats, single elderly people 51 – Council terraces, unemployment, many singles 52 – Council flats, single parents, unemployment
	High rise hardship	53 – Old people in high rise flats 54 – Singles and single parents, high rise estates
	Inner city adversity	55 – Multi-ethnic, purpose built estates 56 – Multi-ethnic, crowded flats

Other examples include car purchase. What may have been a status purchase in the past may now take on a new dimension. Increasingly, segments of purchasers are interested in the cars fuel consumption, its CO_2 emissions as well as its performance and style.

Behavioural Segmentation

The segmentation variables that have been considered have been customer centric in order that the marketer develops as complete a profile as possible on each individual. Behavioural segmentation looks at building relationships with the individual.

> Research by a major UK issuer of credit cards found that in the early stages of the relationship, the customer was wary about telephoning the card issuer if they had any concerns about the cards or how it should be used. The solution was to provide new customers with dedicated helpline number that identified them. The call centre staff having been alerted to the status of the customer was able to be more understanding of their situation.

Behavioural segmentation can be categorised into:

- End-use
- Benefits sought

Increasing use is being made of behavioural segmentation, and we will look at two examples.

End-use

The purpose that the product will be used for dramatically changes the way the product is marketed.

Brands and products have been developed to reflect the use of the product.

A hotel may market itself as a conference venue during the week reflecting the quality of the accommodation, the dedicated business centre within the hotel with access to administrative support, free Internet access for delegates, photocopying and state-of-the-art IT equipment.

At weekends where there are no conferences taking place, the emphasis may now be on the leisure facilities, the relaxing atmosphere and the quality of service.

A bank manufactures a loan product, which offers a fixed rate of interest and a fixed but variable repayment term.

Interest rate is set at 7.9% APR, and the customer can select a repayment period of between one and seven years.

The bank can market the loan in a variety of ways to reflect product usage.

- For customers looking to buy a car, it can be marketed as a car loan.
- For general purposes, we can call it a personal loan.
- For customers who have been overspending and need money to pay off other debts, it is now a consolidation loan.

Benefits Sought

Consider the purchase of a pair of ladies jeans. Are the jeans being bought for weekend causal wear or are they simply something practical to wear while driving the car or sitting in the garden?

The purchase of convenience meals is increasing in popularity, but how should they be marketed? Are they for lazy people who cannot be bothered to cook for themselves? Or are they a quick and convenient alternative to spending time cooking so that there is more time available for other more interesting activities. Finally, are convenience foods an alternative to a meal out or a takeaway?

Marks & Spencer ran a promotion offering a meal for two at £10, including a bottle of wine, positioning it as a 'good night in'.

Usage Rate

Consumers use products at different rates; usage can be defined as light, medium and heavy. Understanding usage can lead to more effective marketing campaigns or in some cases, migrating customers to more appropriate products.

> Tesco monitors the usage of its Internet shopping service. Regular customers typically make one purchase per week. If after a certain period of time no purchases are made, the customer receives an e-mail offering them some form of incentive to resume shopping. Otherwise, if customers change their purchasing habits, it is harder to encourage repeat purchase.

Loyalty

Customer loyalty can be a helpful segmentation variable, but brand loyalty can be fragile. Many organisations operate loyalty programmes or cards, but how many loyalty cards do we carry around with us?

It can be helpful for an organisation to understand whether customers are:

- Loyal to use
- Loyal to others
- Switchers

Knowing which group a customer occupies allows them to be targeted.

Attitude

Customers may buy from an organisation for a number of reasons. The customer who buys electricity from a particular power company may not feel any loyalty or enthusiasm towards the company. Similarly, the credit card user who has a large credit balance on the card that attracts a high rate of interest is not going to feel as enthusiastic, towards the organisation as the customer who pays off debt every month and sees the card as a great way to manage money effectively.

Buyer Readiness

Customers go through various stages to make a purchase (awareness, interest, desire, action: AIDA) and organisations need to recognise and respond differently to the customers in the various stages of purchase.

International Segmentation

Geographic segmentation is clearly an important part of international segmentation. Some of the world's largest organisations will have a physical presence in key world markets as well as operating in literally hundreds of countries.

International segmentation benefits from a multivariable approach, and it is not always distance from the home country that is important. France is the UKs nearest neighbour, and it could be argued that culturally the UK is closer to Hong Kong (an old UK colony), some 6,000 miles away.

All countries, even those grouped together regionally (e.g. Europe) can exhibit significant differences, not only in economic terms but culturally and politically. To address this, international segmentation requires world markets to be grouped into segments with distinct buying needs and behaviours.

For the UK, we have discussed ACORN as a way of segmenting consumers; Europe has similar tools including CCN EuroMOSAIC. Business segmentation uses SIC classification and the USA operates the North American Industrial Classification System (NAICS).

While geographic segmentation may be a good start point (acknowledging the problems mentioned earlier), it should also be recognised that incomes vary from country to country along with buying patterns, lifestyle, education and behaviour patterns.

Segments can be based around, for example, cultural dimensions; countries can be grouped together where the beliefs, values, religion and customers are similar and alternatively segments can be grouped together around political structures.

Another dimension to consider is that of global similarities. The Disney Channel targets young children and teenagers across the globe with the same films and TV programmes. Similarly MTV, attracts the same teenage segment worldwide and brands such as Nike offer the same advertising messages worldwide: 'Just do It'.

Organisations like IKEA adopted an interesting approach to new markets. Generally regarded as a truly global company, IKEA targeted specific market segments, irrespective of the country in which they were located (intermarket segmentation). For example, young professionals and families would be similarly segmented in France, Italy, UK, etc.

ACTIVITY 9.3

Identify different ways in which the market for personal laptop computers could be segmented?

We have looked at the different ways in which markets can be segmented. The point must be made that organisations, due to the levels and availability of high quality data are moving away where possible from single variable segmentation to multivariable segmentation, which will improve a company's competitive advantage.

Multivariable segmentation while having many advantages such as being able to build a highly sophisticated profile on individuals and groups of individuals also provides an organisation with a much wider range of segmentation options. As we will see later, effective segmentation relies on financial viability, i.e. when an organisation evaluates a segment it will want to know that it going to be financially rewarded. Therefore, a balance will need to be struck on the level of segmentation desirable with the income to be generated.

CRITERIA FOR EFFECTIVE SEGMENTATION

To even get attention, a segment must fulfil a number of criteria.

Measurable

The segment must be capable of being measured. This is usually a straightforward procedure with the data being available internally to the organisation or from external secondary sources. Primary data may need to be commissioned if insufficient data is available.

Accessible

Having identified the segment, has the organisation got the financial, or other resources to exploit the segment.

Substantial

The availability of data can lead an organisation to identify small segments, which in fact may be too small and therefore not cost effective. Segments can be aggregated to make them larger or ignored. Size is of course relative to the organisation undertaking the analysis.

Unique

The segment should be such that it can be specifically identified.

Appropriate

The segment should satisfy the organisation's mission, vision and objectives and support the brand values.

Stable

The future performance of the segment should be capable of being forecast with some degree of accuracy. Having invested in the segment, there is an expectation of future returns.

Attracting and Retaining the Right Customers (Relationship-Based Segmentation)

In unprecedented market conditions, balancing risk and reward is becoming critical in the financial services market. Lenders' attraction and retention strategies are being scrutinised by a multitude of stakeholders including the Bank of England, the Treasury and the FSA as well as ordinary investors and indeed the public at large. It is, therefore, essential that attraction and retention is optimised so as to maximise profitability, optimise operational costs and minimise risk, whilst carefully utilising resources and capital funding – all of course within the backdrop of TCF.

Attracting and retaining the right customers are inextricably linked because establishing the right method of attracting customers will lead to solid customer retention. A long-term strategy of attracting and retaining the right customer can have a positive impact on many factors and, ultimately, will result in a more profitable mortgage book.

The use of data and technology

Until recently, attracting customers has not been a difficult task for any lender in terms of business volume. However, apart from risk assessments (which are, of course, essential), all customers had virtually been treated to the same service, processes, sales channels, products and more or less the same pricing. Recent events have, however, caused most lenders to ask whether they had been targeting the right customers?

We have all heard much about pricing for risk but what about 'price-for-good-risk' or 'right customer, right price'? Up until now, many lenders have largely failed to build into their customer attraction strategies factors such as customer profitability, future potential and cross-sale propensity.

One of the reasons why this has been so difficult to achieve in the past is the availability of accurate and timely data. Available information has often been historic and out of date and has, therefore, not been current enough to make real-time decisions.

Advances in data collection and manipulation models have been significant in recent times, and modern technology systems now allow this data to be brought easily into the sales process in real-time. Not only does this help assess the right risk and detect fraud but it also helps with more accurate pricing (down to individual customer level), the maximising of every opportunity and the ability to increase cross-sales significantly. Thus the customer receives not only a better and more relevant product offering but it can be achieved using a single application process, which is both cheaper for the lender and more user-friendly for the customer.

Take, for example, cross-selling and a potential solution; your point-of-sale system uses the appropriate data model to identify that the 'right' customer is going through the sales process. The data model identifies that a number of cross-sale opportunities exist for other credit-related products and related protection products. The point-of-sale system uses this data and the data captured during the mortgage application process to present the customer with pre-approved options and a pricing 'bundle' – using an approach similar to that of Amazon books. In the background, the system has populated all relevant application forms and all that is required from the customer is an acceptance.

In summary, it is a matter of using data and technology to identify the customer type, in real-time, present the relevant cross-sale, which has been priced and pre-approved, and reuse all the data to make the buying and application process as quick and as simple as possible.

It is also important to note that, in current market conditions, this can be achieved without the need for a large IT spend and protracted delivery timescales. For example, modern point-of-sale platforms are able to bolt on to lenders' existing components and systems without the need for a costly re-platforming of the whole technology infrastructure.

So what about retaining the right customers? At this unprecedented time of decimated mortgage lending and declining house prices, it may seem somewhat optimistic to be discussing borrower retention. However, those of us who have experienced other challenging times in the market will know that, at some point, a corner will be turned. When recovery does begin, it is likely that the mortgage market will improve before the housing market and this is certainly where competition will appear first, with lenders attempting to cherry-pick each other's back book. Once again, retention strategies will be important as lenders will have to ensure that they are protecting their best borrowers while retaining margin as much as possible.

In order to identify and to help retain the right customers, Experian has developed a suite of solutions focussing on the mortgage market; these utilise the breadth of Experian's data assets, including credit bureau data and the consumer dynamics data resource.

One element of this is a revolutionary tool which uses a series of scores, generated from real-time consumers' credit behaviours and activity, including external databases that monitor indebtedness, affordability, property indexing, profit forecasting and future opportunity modelling. The result is a tool that provides an effective mechanism to help lenders identify customers who present an attrition risk and take necessary retention activity if they have been identified as the right customer.

Moving forward, a combination of data and technology will not only be essential for attracting and retaining, but will also play a key role in deciding how best to service customers to optimise profitability and operational efficiency. Multichannel distribution will become as much lender as customer driven. As with the investment industry, clients will be serviced differently depending on their complexity and profitability. For this reason, brokers will always be a part of the industry, but equally, more savvy clients may choose to move online because of pricing differentiation or convenience. This presents both a challenge for lenders, but also an opportunity, as consumer direct channels allow lenders to be more in control of the customer sales process, in particular allowing lenders to control pricing, cross-selling and the use and reuse of data more easily. It could be a very exciting time ahead for the industry.

When attracting the right customers, lenders may ask:

'How do I secure more profitable customers – at a decent price and for the right risk?' The answer: individual product pricing; better use of consumer data; product differentiation; holistic cross-selling capability, and channel operational optimisation.

Or

'How do I make the most out of every sale?' The answer: make the initial/primary sale as efficient as possible; present relevant other product offerings; reuse data; one application process, and price bundling.

When retaining the right customers, lenders may ask:

'How do I know which customers not to retain?' The answer: use external data, for example, indebtedness, affordability, property indexing, profit forecasting and future opportunity.

Or

'How do I retain customers more cost effectively?' The answer: process automation; a self-service retention channel; customer segmentation, and effective use of appropriate resources and channel.

The combination of data and technology can provide a powerful weapon in the quest for retaining and attracting the right customers and ensuring that lenders meet the tighter regulatory and investor requirements that are guaranteed to be a result of the current and unprecedented happenings in the mortgage market.

Source: http://www.experian.co.uk/www/pages/downloads/productSheets/attracting-and-retaining-right-customers.pdf

QUESTIONS

1. Give a definition of marketing strategy.
2. What do you understand by the term market segmentation?
3. Outline the eight stages of the STP process.
4. What are the benefits of segmentation?
5. What do you understand by macrosegmentation?
6. What ways can consumer markets be segmented?
7. How can international markets be segmented?
8. What are the criteria for effective segmentation?

SUMMARY

This chapter has introduced the role of marketing strategies in marketing planning and has focussed on the STP process. The benefits of segmentation have been outlined and the different variables, both the B2B and the B2C markets, have been explored. It should be appreciated that segmentation is complex and requires a detailed understanding of customers and customer behaviour. Some segmentation variables focus on market characteristics, whereas others are more concerned with product usage and buyer behaviour.

Increasingly sophisticated segmentation variables are combined to develop a detailed profile of segments which is then used to offer particular products to the customer in order to retain them and generate additional income. For most organisations, segmentation is an important strategy as it recognises that not all customers are equal and different approaches need to be adopted depending on value that each segment is worth to the organisation. Moreover, organisations do not have finite resources and, therefore, they must be used to their best advantage by identifying the most valuable segments to be targeted.

BIBLIOGRAPHY

Dibb, S., Simpkin, L., Pride, W. and Ferrell, O.C. (2006) *'Marketing: Concepts and Strategies*, 5th edition. Houghton Mifflin, Boston.

Doyle, P. (1994) *Marketing Management and Strategy*. Prentice Hall, Hemel Hempstead.

Smith, W. (1956) Product Differentiation and Market Segmentation as Alternative Marketing Strategies. *Journal of Marketing*, July, 3–8.

CHAPTER 10

Market Targeting

3.4 Assess the value of 'targeting' markets as an approach to achieving customer satisfaction, competitive advantage and retention
3.5 Critically evaluate a range of targeting coverage strategies for different organisational contexts and sectors
3.6 Assess the attractiveness and value of selected market segments

SYLLABUS REFERENCES

3.4:

- focused effort and resource efficiency
- potential for achieving short, medium and long-term objectives
- potential for achieving competitive advantage
- scope for competitive advantage through distinctive positioning

3.5:

- undifferentiated marketing
- differentiated marketing
- concentrated marketing
- customised marketing

3.6:

- external and internal criteria for evaluation: size, growth, profitability, relationship potential, competition and capabilities
- segment evaluation process: factor weighting and ranking of alternatives
- fit between potential and internal considerations

INTRODUCTION

Having decided on a segmentation strategy in order to break the market down into more manageable and effective segments, the next stage in the process is to approach the target sub-markets with a distinctive approach.

A target market is recognised as a set of buyers sharing common needs or characteristics that the company decides to serve.

In an ideal world because each buyer has a unique requirement, a separate marketing mix would be designed for each. In reality, organisations generally target buyers broadly, narrowly or somewhere in the middle. This is known as undifferentiated, concentrated and differentiated targeting strategies(Figure 10.1).

FIGURE 10.1

Targeting Strategies

TARGETING STRATEGIES

Undifferentiated

In an undifferentiated strategy, the organisation treats the whole market as being homogenous. No significant differences are perceived between the different buyers and so the organisation uses just one marketing mix to engage with the entire market.

Marketing mix ⟶ Market

Although this approach offers the advantages of cost and mass appeal, it clearly cannot suit the entire market, and it can be argued that sales will be lost. Competitors who have a more focussed approach could be stealing business away. It is an approach usually associated with low involvement in the purchase process.

Some commentators argue that an undifferentiated approach is rarely possible and examples such as the purchase of potatoes and salt are often citied.

No longer do we just buy a potato, we can choose from salad, baking, roasting, chipping or mashing. This makes the 'regular' or general purpose potatoes look like an inferior product.

Some organisations adopt an undifferentiated approach because they are small players in a small market.

Differentiated

Marketing mix 1	⟶	Market segment 1
Marketing mix 2	⟶	Market segment 2
Marketing mix 3	⟶	Market segment 3
Marketing mix 4	⟶	Market segment 4

A differentiated strategy requires an organisation to develop a different marketing mix for each segment. So, each of the market segments served by the organisation will receive a different offer.

Royal Bank of Scotland (RBS) operates a number of insurance brands including Tesco, Direct Line, Privilege NatWest and Churchill. Each brand approaches the customer in a different way to increase the appeal.

As organisations increasingly appeal to wider, more diverse and overseas markets, then the range of marketing mixes used has to be increased to reflect the needs of the customers.

Airlines will want to appeal to different classes of traveller from economy to economy plus, through to business and first class.

Universities are differentiating the marketing mix to reflect the needs of undergraduate, postgraduate and professional students, which can then be grouped into EU and overseas students.

Cadburys the chocolate manufacturer bought Green and Black's, an upmarket and organic brand, to serve the needs of a growing market segment.

Concentrated

Marketing mix 1	⟶	Market segment 2

In a concentrated strategy, the organisation concentrates on serving just one segment of the market developing expertise and a highly detailed knowledge of the market in which just one marketing mix is used. The target market will see the organisation as the leader in the field giving it advantages over other more general competitors.

Concentrated marketing works best in niche segments which tend on average to be small so the mix tends to be highly focused.

Rolls Royce the car manufacturer aims its vehicles in the affluent sector and does not compete with General Motors.

Steinway pianos produce handmade pianos which take over 12 months to build and only focus on the concert hall and celebrity markets.

Rolex the watch manufacture targets wealthy individuals and does not compete with Timex who produces an inexpensive and functional range of watches.

Although the advantages of a concentrated strategy may be clear, it can bring disadvantages in the sense that if the segment fails to perform, the organisation will not be able to move easily into another segment.

The growing appeal of the Internet with low set-up cost will increasingly make concentrated marketing more appealing to organisations of all sizes, something which the larger organisations will be monitoring carefully.

ROLEX WATCHES

Rolex SA was founded in 1905 by Hans Wilsdorf and his brother-in-law, Alfred Davis.

Wilsdorf & Davis was the original name of what later became the Rolex Watch Company. They originally imported Hermann Aegler's Swiss movements to England and placed them in quality cases made by Dennison and others. These early wristwatches were then sold to jewellers, who then put their own names on the dial. The earliest watches from the firm of Wilsdorf and Davis are usually marked "W&D" – inside the caseback only.

Hans Wilsdorf registered the trademark name 'Rolex' in La Chaux-de-Fonds, Switzerland during 1908. The word was made up, but its origin is obscure. A rumour never substantiated is that the word 'Rolex' came from the French phrase horlogerie exquise, meaning exquisite watch industry.

The Wilsdorf & Davis company moved out of Great Britain in 1912. From that time until 2007, Rolex has been headquartered in Geneva, Switzerland, though the company owns facilities in other world markets. In 2007, Rolex moved its headquarters to the USA.

The company name Rolex was registered on 15 November 1915. Wilsdorf's desire was for the brand to be easily pronounceable in any language. The company name was officially changed to the Rolex Watch Company during 1919. It was later changed to Montres Rolex, SA and finally Rolex, SA.

Rolex SA is a foundation initiated and originally funded by Hans Wilsdorf and the Aegler family. According to foundation documentation, the Rolex SA company can never be sold nor traded on any stock market.

Today Rolex manufactures watches and other accessories and is generally considered a status symbol and a sign of significant wealth. It is the worlds largest luxury watch brand and one of the world-leading global brands and the number one brand for watches.

Rolex.com

The Table 10.1 highlights the advantages and disadvantages of each of the strategies.

ALTERNATIVE TARGETING APPROACHES

In addition to the above strategies, the concept of micromarketing, which refers to the practice of tailoring products and programmes to meet the

Table 10.1 Advantages and Disadvantages of Targeting Strategies

Undifferentiated

Advantages	Disadvantages
■ Economies of scale maximised ■ Cost of marketing and production minimised	■ Organisation may only be of general interest to the buyers, with few showing a particular interest ■ Buyers may prefer organisations specialising in their particular segment(s)

Concentrated

Advantages	Disadvantages
■ Organisation gains detailed knowledge of the segment ■ Specialism can be very profitable	■ The organisation has a heavy dependency on one segment which may not be sustainable in the long term

Differentiated

Advantages	Disadvantages
■ Organisation tailors the marketing mix to the needs of the segment	■ Additional costs incurred as a result of the differentiation process ■ Economies of scale opportunities lost ■ Organisational resources maybe spread thinly

needs of individuals and locations, may be considered as an alternative strategy.

Micromarketing is about seeing an individual in every customer and not a customer in every individual, and includes local and individual marketing.

Micromarketing is a form of target marketing in which companies tailor their marketing programmes to the needs and wants of a narrowly defined geographic, demographic, psychographic or behavioural segments.

Local marketing involves tailoring brands and promotions to the needs and wants of local customer groups.

Tesco the UKs leading food retailer offers its customers a range of store formats for different locations, but within each of the formats, the store can carry an individual product range suited to local customer needs.

Tesco is an international retailer, and wherever it operates, it focusses on giving local customers what they want.

Store Formats

They have four different store formats, each tailored to their customers' needs and one trial format called Homeplus.

Express (Up to 3,000 sq ft)

Their Express stores offer customers great value, quality and fresh food close to where they live and work. They opened their first Express store in 1994. They sell a range of up to 7,000 products including fresh produce, wines and spirits and in-store bakery.

Metro (Approximately 7,000–15,000 sq ft)

They opened their first Metro in 1992, bringing the convenience of Tesco to town and city centre locations. Metros cater for thousands of busy customers each week and offer a tailored range of mainly food products, including ready meals and sandwiches.

Superstore (Approximately 20,000–50,000 sq ft)

They began opening Superstores in the 1970s and during the 1980s and 1990s built a national network, to which they are adding every year. They have an ongoing programme of extending and refreshing their superstores to improve the overall experience for customers. In recent years, they have introduced a number of new non-food ranges into superstores such as DVDs and books.

Extra (Approximately 60,000 sq ft and Above)

Since opening their first Extra in 1997, the one-stop destination store has proved extremely popular. Extra stores offer the widest range of food and non-food lines, ranging from electrical equipment to homewares, clothing, health and beauty, and seasonal items such as garden furniture.

Homeplus (Approximately 35,000–50,000 sq ft)

Their Homeplus stores are dedicated to non-food, including clothing. These trial stores offer their widest range of non-food products in store, with more available through their Tesco Direct order and collection points. Their latest, largest stores have their Tesco Direct catalogue ranges on display, with most products available to take home today. Following the early promise of the first seven stores, they have committed to opening a further ten as part of the trial.

Understanding our customers

Tesco Clubcard is a world-leading loyalty card scheme, with around 14 million active cardholders. Information provided by Clubcard enables them to better understand their customers and say 'thank you' for shopping with them. There are over 8 million unique coupon variations with each Clubcard mailing, making sure that everyone receives the kind of offer that is appropriate for them.

http://www.tescoplc.com/plc/about_us/strategy/coreuk/

Individual Marketing

Increased sophistication of marketing (see Tesco example above) offers organisations the opportunity to offer customers an 'individual' product.

ACTIVITY 10.1

For an automobile manufacturer of your choice, select just one model of car. Identify how many different options that 'one' model can be built with. Why do think there are so many options?

The choice of which targeting strategy to use is influenced by a number of factors which are driven both internally and externally within the organisation.

- Resources available – It may be more effective for an organisation to utilise limited resources on developing one segment.

- The nature of the market – It may be homogeneous and therefore it may be more attractive to develop just one broad approach. However, as we will see below, markets are increasingly being broken into much smaller segments, which may make this approach unwise in many and increasing circumstances.

- The competition – How is it targeting the market and is there the opportunity for a different approach?

- Product life cycle stage – At product launch stage an organisation will often launch just one product variant and as the competition enters the markets, other variants may be needed. Similarly, as the product reaches maturity, product variations can increase the life cycle.

Socially Responsible Consequences of Target Marketing

Social responsibility is concerned with an organisation's duty to maximise its positive impact and minimise its negative impact on society: customers, the environment and the wider community.

Targeted marketing, if planned and well executed, will enable an organisation to maximise revenue from the segment(s) and lead to greater customer satisfaction as their needs will have met more effectively.

However, over the years different market industry sectors have variously been accused of targeting vulnerable segments which can include the elderly infirm and children. In many cases, legislation has been introduced in the UK and overseas to ensure that target marketing is appropriate.

It is not just the vulnerable sectors which come in for criticism, sometimes boundaries are not clear. In the UK, the introduction of 'Alcopops' caused controversy; the drink came in a variety of sweet flavours such as blackcurrant and although high in alcohol, didn't actually taste alcoholic. Arguments were founded on the fact that the drink had strong appeal to under 18s, although legally they could not buy it.

Smoking advertisements are now banned from appearing on the TV in the UK and the ongoing issue of 'junk food' is being addressed through government awareness campaigns in a similar way to alcohol.

The Internet as a new medium has yet to be fully regulated and organisations continue to use this media to target special segments.

In conclusion, the issue which must be deal with is how and what to target, i.e. the manner and the nature of the product involved rather than who is being targeted.

EVALUATING MARKET SEGMENTS

We have identified that markets can be 'oversegmented', which not only affects organisational profitability but also has the potential to confuse customers by trying to place them in a segment they cannot relate to or understand.

Banks often categorise business into turnover bands.

- Up to £1m (small)
- £1−10m (medium)
- £10m + (large)

Many businesses that had a turnover in excess of £1m felt they were a small business and could not relate to the banks segmentation policy.

Decisions therefore need to be made as to which market segments to target based upon some rationale.

To evaluate the potential of market segments, two issues are to be identified.

- The market attractiveness of the various segments
- The organisation's ability to meet the needs of the segments

In addressing these issues, the competition, market factors and environmental considerations need to be taken into account.

The Competition

- Bargaining power of the suppliers
- Bargaining power of the buyers
- Barriers to entry
- Likelihood of new entrants
- Cost of leaving the market

You may remember the above considerations as Porter's Five Forces analysis. In addition, the strength, numbers and nature of the competition needs to be understood.

Market Factors

- How big is the segment now and likely to be in the future?

- How will customers react to price changes, i.e. does the segment offer price elasticity or inelasticity?

- Are there seasonal patterns which will affect demand?

- Stage in the industry life cycle, declining industries will be short lived and drain resources quickly. Conversely, new industries, e.g. telecoms will be cash hungry at the outset with the potential for strong financial rewards in the longer term.

Environmental Factors

These are based on a PESTEL analysis and could include the following.

- Political changes – What changes are likely, nationally and internationally? Increased levels of political risk will make certain segments less attractive.

- Economic – Will the reduced levels of credit and savings affect the market? The ageing nature of the UK population is encouraging growth in certain segments.

- Social – Lifestyle changes open up new markets.

- Technology – What substitute products will technological changes bring?

- Environmental – What changes will 'green' issues bring about and how will this affect competition within the segment?

- Legal – Are there any legal issues, which may affect the segment? The requirement for all homes to have a House owner Information Pack (HIP) when the property is being sold opened up a new industry in the UK.

The shell directional policy matrix has been adapted to apply to market segmentation and the adapted matrix is shown in Figure 10.2.

The axis shows two dimensions:

■ Market attractiveness
■ Strengths of the organisation in serving the segment

Market segment attractiveness

	Unattractive	Average	Attractive
Weak	Strongly avoid	Avoid	Possibilities
Average	Avoid	Possibilities	Secondary targets
Strong	Possibilities	Secondary targets	Prime targets

Strengths (Current & potential company strengths in serving segment)

The nine cells in the matrix offer different opportunities, so placing a segment in the appropriate cell provides a guide to the attractiveness of the segment.

The market attractiveness criteria which we identified earlier can then be 'weighted' by the organisation relative to its importance as defined by the organisation (Table 10.2).

Table 10.2 Market Attractiveness Criteria	
Criteria	**Weighting (%)**
Profit potential	60
Market growth rate	20
Market size	10
Strength of competition	10

The same process is used to identify the strengths of the organisation relevant to the sector (Table 10.3).

This process ensures that each organisation using the matrix adopts a unique approach and identifies the attractiveness from its own perspective. It therefore follows that different organisations will come to different conclusions about the attractiveness of particular market segments.

Table 10.3	Business Strengths Criteria
Criteria	**Weighting (%)**
Market share	60
Potential for differential advantage	20
Potential cost advantages	10
Brand image	10

Using the weighted approach will identify segments for priority and, in effect, acts as a screening process. The approach, while clearly identifying the key segments to target, and avoid, allows the middle segments, i.e. possibilities to be developed or ignored in accordance with their ranking.

ACTIVITY 10.2

How does each of the main supermarkets in your country segment their markets? What criteria do you think they use to evaluate target markets?

QUESTIONS

1. Explain how a company can identify attractive market segments and choose a market targeting strategy?

2. What are the main advantages of a concentrated marketing strategy?

3. What impact do you think the Internet will have on the choice of market strategy?

4. What do you understand by the term 'local' marketing?

5. What issues can arise as a result of socially responsible target marketing?

SUMMARY

This chapter has explored the concept of market targeting, i.e. identifying a particular market segment and tailoring the marketing approach to the segment. Three different approaches have been identified, illustrated and evaluated. The competitive environment is increasingly moving organisations towards adopting a more differentiated approach, recognising that not all customers have the same needs and wants and that competitive advantage can be gained through targeting. Customers are looking for specific solutions to their problems rather than having to work out for themselves whether a generic solution can be adapted for their needs. The way in which alternative market segments may be evaluated for targeting is then considered using a set of criteria based on external and internal factors.

BIBLIOGRAPHY

Kotler, P. and Keller, K.L. (2006) *Marketing Management*, 12th edition. Prentice Hall, Englewood Cliffs, NJ.

Kotler, P., Armstrong, G., Wong, V. and Saunders, J. (2008) *Principles of Marketing*, 5th edition. Financial Times/Prentice Hall, Harlow.

Marketing Positioning

3.7 Examine the concept of marketing positioning strategy and how it can be used to convey the organisation's value proposition

3.8 Critically evaluate positioning options and their implementation within the context of the organisation and its markets

3.7:

- differential advantage, customer value and organisational benefits
- consideration of alternative positioning strategies
- relationship positioning strategies
- competitive positioning strategies
- selection of target markets and point of differentiation
- positioning and perceptual maps

3.8:

- criteria for effective positioning and competitive advantage
- positioning and the marketing mix
- positioning and repositioning in practice

INTRODUCTION

Having segmented the market as part of its overall strategy, an organisation will then identify selected target segments within the market where it wants to compete for business. Then, as the final stage of the STP process, it will need to position itself very clearly in the minds of customers, so the organisation, its products or its brands will be selected rather than competitor offerings.

POSITIONING

The organisation will want to develop and maintain a competitive (differential) advantage compared with the completion.

Differential advantage is an attribute of the brand, product, service or marketing mix that is desired by the targeted customer and provided by only one supplier.

Dibb et al. (2006)

An organisation needs to have a competitive or differential advantage over its rivals which can be actual or perceived by the customers, and this can be achieved through the organisation balancing the needs of the customer with the resources available.

Competitive positioning has been defined as 'the act of designing the company's offer and image so that they occupy a meaningful and distinctive position in the target customer's mind'.

Kotler and Keller (2006)

To be successful, today's organisations needs to be market orientated which requires them to strike a balance between customer and competitor focus. No longer can an organisation simply monitor the competition and then develop a response. Focus needs to be on understanding the needs of the customer and building profitable and long-lasting relationships through innovative strategies, which will deliver greater customer value than the competition is able to offer.

Positioning and competition can take place at the following levels:

- Company
- Product
- Brand

A supermarket can appeal to customers in a variety of ways: price, product range, freshness and so on. Customers will choose that particular supermarket because they know or believe it will meet their needs.

In the example above, a customer would be making a choice based on the overall positioning of the organisation. But positioning can occur at product level; a customer looking to purchase a new TV may be evaluating a Samsung product against a Sony. Similarly, at brand level how does Coca-Cola position itself against Pepsi or Virgin Cola?

These considerations are important and can allow an organisation to move successfully into other markets.

Tesco has slogan 'Every Little Helps' and along with its strong brand name this has allowed it to move beyond food retailing into financial services, petrol, clothing, opticians and so on.

Criteria to Create Differentiation

It is the case that not all competitive differences will create strong competitive positions and Kotler and Keller (2006) suggest criteria which should be applied in an effort to create differentiation. The Table 11.1 is based around these criteria.

Perceptual maps are used to identify consumer's perceptions of a product or brand and the position occupied in the market as measured by set criteria.

Competitive positioning has already been identified as the act of designing the company's offer and image so that they occupy a meaningful and distinctive position in the target customer's mind. For example, in the car market, Volvo may have an association with safety and Skoda may be associated with value for money.

Dibb et al. (2006) suggest that a positioning is not what is done to the product, but what is created in the mind of the consumer and therefore elements of the process are outside the control of the organisation. Skoda in the above example may score well when measured as value for money, but may not be purchased because for social reasons, i.e. it is perceived as 'inferior'.

It has been argued that the brand operates at two levels:

1. Functional, i.e. what the product does
2. Emotional, i.e. what the product means

Table 11.1   Criteria for Differentiation
Importance – The point or points of difference should be readily appreciated and understood by the majority of customers.
Profitability – The costs involved in developing the differentiation will be rewarded through being able to charge a price sufficient to repay the cost of investment and generate profits.
Distinctive – The product cannot be copied or performed better by others.
Superior – The difference must offer the customer a better way to receive the expected benefits.
Affordable – Customers can and are willing to pay for the product.
Communicable – The difference can easily be communicated and understood by customers.

In the Skoda example, the car may appeal at the functional level, but be rejected at the emotional level.

Organisations can adopt a number of positioning characteristics which helps to position the brand in the consumer's mind.

Some positioning examples:

Qantas airline – The spirit of Australia
Flybe airline – Book with confidence
Smooth radio – Lose yourself
Neilson travel – Meet someone new on holiday

Upshaw (1995) identified the following different types of positioning prompts (Table 11.2).

Table 11.2	Positioning Prompts
Feature driven	The specific features of the product are used to differentiate it, e.g. bagless, cordless, wireless.
Problem solution	Unique solution to the problem 'the product actually works'.
Target driven	The nature of the consumer identifies a place in the market, e.g. 'people like you'.
Competitive driven	A position taken against the competition is established, e.g. BA and Virgin.
Emotional	Charities often add emotion to their brand
Benefit driven	The benefits to be gained from the product, e.g. Virgin Airlines' Business class offers a taxi to pick up from home or office.
Aspiration	Successful people use this brand
Value	Aldi or ASDA, e.g. use this positioning

BRAND POSITIONING

Product positioning starts with the product and brand positioning 'starts with establishing a frame of reference, which signals to consumers the goal they can expect to receive by using a brand' (Yeshin, 2006). The frame of reference can often be other brands in the same category, e.g. Hugo Boss or Ted Baker. Alternatively, the frame can be in different sectors, e.g. Virgin trains and Easyjet where both offer travel solutions.

Kotler et al. (2008) suggested a brand could be positioned according to a range of associations (Table 11.3).

Table 11.3	Brand Associations
Attributes	Solvent free, no hydrogenate fat or GM ingredients
Benefits	Safety and durability
Occasion	Opening hours, Christmas, holidays, etc.
Users	Environmentally friendly
Activity	Sport or relaxation
Personality	Churchill Insurance
Origin	British heritage or German engineering
Symbol	Microsoft logo, NatWest logo
Product class	Morning goods, personal hygiene products
Competition	Positioned as 'Reassuringly Expensive' but not best in class in blind tasting sessions

Organisations need to decide carefully how they want to position their products compared to the competition. To aid the selection process (Jobber, 2007) identified four key factors critical to the process (Table 11.4).

Table 11.4	Positioning Factors
Credence	Attributes used by the organisation to position the product must be credible, e.g. the BMW 3 Series Coupe with sports suspension offers 58.9 miles to a gallon of petrol is credible. Suggesting a Range Rover offers fuel efficiency would be difficult to justify.
Competitiveness	The product must offer benefits not provided by the competition. Tradition, prestige and superiority of Oxbridge colleges compared with other universities.
Consistency	Lloyds TSB has used 'with you for the journey' to demonstrate it wants to maintain a consistent positioning.
Clarity	Clear position 'no nasty stuff' or 'it does what it says on the tin'.

PERCEPTUAL MAPS

These represent different brands in relation to each other based on some key distinguishing factors in the market. The Figure 11.1 represents a simple perceptual map of various airlines. The attributes identified through market research are price and perceived overall quality in this case, but a range of other attributes such as service standards or reliability could have been used.

FIGURE 11.1

Perceptual Map of Airlines

Each circle in the map shows the brand's perceived position mapped against two variables of quality and price. The size of each circle represents the relative market share held by the brand. We can see that in the low price/ high quality quadrant that two brands are competing and brand '6' has the higher market share.

Where the circles are located close together customers see the brand as being similar when viewed against the two variables. Measurement against other attributes would show a different perception and therefore different relative position.

By positioning the brand in accordance with one of the criteria outlined above the organisation is raising the customer's expectation on the nature of the product and offering. Failure to deliver on these promises will bring the inevitable consequences of failure.

The perceptual map shown is based on customer perception, but an alternative approach would have to develop the map based on the competition. This approach allows an organisation to develop a deeper understanding of the competition and from the basis of a strategy to attack or defend positions depending on the strength of the competition.

In the low price/low quality market only brand '8' is competing and there is potentially a gap in the market where an organisation may potentially want to compete because there is no existing competition and it represents the ideal positioning, i.e. relatively low price, with relatively low quality.

ACTIVITY 11.1

For a market of your choice, develop a perceptual map showing the relative positioning of the competing brands based upon two key attributes on which customers distinguish between them. Identify whether there are any potential gaps in the market.

POSITIONING ALTERNATIVES

Perceptual maps are based on research so that the resultant map produced has validity and the organisation has confidence in the findings. However, Ries and Trout (1981) identified three alternative positioning approaches (Table 11.5):

1. Distinctive attributes
2. Unoccupied positions
3. Repositioning

LEEDS COLLEGE OF MUSIC

Leeds College of Music (LCM) is regarded as a dynamic and progressive institution. It boasts an impressive list of alumni and substantial performance facilities.

For some time, there has been a disparity between LCM's reputation and its outward image. With strong competition coming from music conservatories and universities, it needs to achieve 'stand out' in a crowded market.

In 2005, Thompson Brand Partners created a distinctive brand identity which reflected the energy, ethos and experience of the institution.

In 2008, LCM topped the national league tables for having the biggest annual rise in UCAS applications.

THE MARKETING MIX

As a result of developing the perceptual map, the organisation may need to change or fine tune its positioning in the market.

Brand positioning is not set in stone and can be changed. We have already mentioned Skoda and following its purchase by Volkswagen, it has been repositioned in the market very successfully.

Table 11.5	Positioning Approaches
Distinctive attributes	
An organisation can seek to build on a current position and create a clear position for the brand. For example, John Lewis the Department store is 'never knowingly underpriced'.	
Unoccupied positions	
The example above suggests that the market has an opportunity for a relatively low-priced airline offering relatively low quality. This may be in the short haul market, where passengers are focussed on price and not too bothered about quality.	
Repositioning	
As the product moves through the PLC physical changes may become necessary to extend its life, e.g. new features. Alternatively, it may be possible to reposition the brand in the minds of customers or potential customers by suggesting a new use, benefit or advantage.	

If we look at our original perceptual map and now add in the ideal position of reasonable price and quality, we can see (Figure 11.1) some brands are some distance way from this position which may account for the 'gap' in the market . Brand 8 is considered to be of poor quality, which is reflected in the price.

While the importance of customer perception has been recognised the marketing mix has a crucial part to play in the positioning process. In addition to the 4Ps identified in Table 11.6 the additional 3Ps of the marketing mix (physical evidence, processes and people) should also be considered as key aspects of positioning.

Table 11.6	The 4Ps and Positioning
Product	■ Are the features and benefits still relevant or do they need to be changed?
	■ Does the branding reflect the products position in the market?
	■ Does the products packaging and presentation reflect in the others aspects of the marketing mix?
	■ Are there new products in the pipeline?
Price	■ Is the price competitive and does it reflect the quality and desirability of the product?
	■ Does the price reflect value for money?
Promotion	■ Does the promotion reflect the positioning and pricing of the product?
	■ Are the right communication channels being used?
Place	■ Are the right distribution channels being used and do they reflect well on the product?
	■ Is the channel structure right?

ACTIVITY 11.2

For each of the additional 3Ps of the extended marketing mix, suggest how they might affect brand positioning. Use real world examples to support your answers.

QUESTIONS

1. Distinguish between functional and emotional attributes of a brand. Use examples from a product or service market of your choice to illustrate this.

2. Explain the importance and use of perceptual maps in the positioning process.

SUMMARY

The focus in this chapter has been on positioning of organisations, products and brands which needs to be supported in the market by an integrated and co-ordinated combination of marketing mix elements. Perceptual maps are a useful tool for comparing relative brand positioning and also for identifying gaps in the market where opportunities may exist. Pursuing these opportunities may provide strategic options for an organisation, which should be evaluated using appropriate internal and external criteria.

BIBLIOGRAPHY

Dibb, S., Simkin, L., Pride, W. and Ferrell, O.C. (2006) *Marketing: Concepts and Strategies*, 5th edition. Houghton Mifflin, Boston.

Jobber, D. (2007) *Principles and Practice of Marketing*, 5th edition. McGraw Hill, Maidenhead.

Kotler, P. and Keller, K.L. (2006) *Marketing Management*, 12th edition. Prentice Hall, Englewood Cliffs, NJ.

Kotler, P., Armstrong, G., Wong, V. and Saunders, J. (2008) *Principles of Marketing*, 5th edition. Financial Times/Prentice Hall, Harlow.

Ries, A. and Trout, J. (1981) *Positioning: The Battle for Your Mind*. McGraw Hill, New York.

Upshaw, L.B. (1995) *Building Brand Identity: A Strategy for Success in a Hostile Marketplace*. John Wiley & Son, New York.

Yeshin, T. (2006) *Advertising*. Thompson, New York.

Senior Examiner's Comments – Section Three

On completion of Section 3, students should have a detailed knowledge and understanding of:

- the nature and purpose of marketing strategies;
- the principle of market STP;
- the different ways in which markets may be segmented and evaluation of these approaches;
- the ways in which effective targeting may take place;
- the positioning of products and services to meet customer requirements.

STP strategies are pivotal to marketing planning in practice as they focus marketing activity on defined audiences that have been selected to fulfil organisational objectives. Thus if students are to be successful in this unit, they need to be fully aware of the way in which strategies are defined in terms of target markets and product offers in different situations.

In order to achieve this, they need to be able to effectively segment markets using a range of variables, profile different customer types and determine an overall targeting strategy. Once segments have been defined in this way, students should gain practical insights into assessing the best markets to target using a set of evaluation criteria. Ultimately, they will be judged on their ability to develop a positioning statement based on target customer requirements using a coherent mix of marketing activities. This needs to be set against a competitive backdrop of gaining advantage over other providers in the same markets, and the way that strategies are based on differential advantage in providing customer value and achieving organisational benefits.

Examples of market segmentation strategy in practice are widely available, and students should also draw upon such activity within their own organisation to help better understand the process. Underpinning the approach that is adopted to understanding more about selecting and delivering offers to target markets should be practical analysis of internal capabilities of the organisation and the relative attractiveness of alternative segments.

Adapting Marketing Planning in Different Contexts

CHAPTER 12

Key Dimensions of Implementing Marketing Planning in Practice

LEARNING OBJECTIVES

4.1 Assess the significance of the key dimensions of implementing marketing planning in practice
4.2 Critically evaluate the barriers and constraints to implementing marketing planning, and consider how they may be addressed by organisations

SYLLABUS REFERENCES

4.1:
- organisational structures, systems and processes
- forecasting and budgeting
- timescales and responsibilities

4.2:
- managerial, organisational and cultural shortcomings
- planning inadequacies
- poor and inadequate organisational resource
- lack of innovation
- failure to integrate into corporate planning systems
- monitoring performance metrics and control mechanisms
- contingency planning
- internal marketing

INTRODUCTION

This chapter covers the part of the syllabus which relates to the critical area of implementing marketing planning. We have seen how a marketing plan is researched, planned and structured. Strategies, marketing programmes and tactics will have been identified and evaluated, but we must now consider the very practical issues surrounding implementation.

In terms of strategy, planning is the easy part, and the real challenge is implementation. The process must be very carefully planned and managed. There are three key areas that are vital to implementation:

1. Communicating the marketing plan across the organisation
2. Specifying the required resources, finance, personnel and time
3. Changes to the organisational structure and culture

A weakness of many marketing plans is the lack of implementation details with the result that not all the planned activities are put into practice. A failure to identify the resources required and the time frame for the activities are typical omissions.

Marketing planning does not end when the marketing plan has been prepared. It is essential that all implementation details are attended to. Even then the process is not complete. The marketing plan document should continue to be updated on an ongoing basis.

Piercy (2002) states that:

'The real strategic problem in marketing is not strategy, it is managing the implementation and change'.

A marketing plan can be prepared with all the correct jargon such as, competitive advantage, market penetration, segmentation, targeting and positioning. However, without implementation the plan will remain simply ideas on a piece of paper.

In terms of strategy, implementation is often the key determinant of success or failure. The history of corporate strategy is littered with examples of great plans but which were failures because of poor implementation. Therefore, implementation should be an integral part of any marketing strategy.

> Never adopt a strategy you do not understand how to implement.

Implementation is critical to the success or failure of any venture and there are some key factors that influence this.

- Strong and committed leadership
- A marketing orientated and customer – focussed culture
- An effective marketing structure
- Adequate resources – both financial and human
- Internal marketing
- Budgets, control and measurement systems

If a strategy is to be successfully executed, it is important that each of these areas is planned and managed effectively.

IMPLEMENTATION

Two dimensions determine the success of a strategy: the strategy itself and the ability to implement it. Bonoma (1984) examined both the appropriateness of strategy and the effectiveness of the skills to implement it (Table 12.1).

Table 12.1	Strategy Implementation	
Success	Appropriate strategy and strong ability to implement	Ideal situation. Few problems
Chance	Inappropriate or poor strategy, lacking detailed analysis, not building on existing strengths. Possibly saved by effective adaptation and execution	How inappropriate is the strategy. What adaptation is possible to the strategy. High risk
Problem	Appropriate strategy, poor implementation	Strength of strategic marketing plan dissipated by poor or inappropriate implementation
Failure	Inappropriate strategy. Lack of ability to implement	Is there any point struggling on with implementation. Quit and avoid further loss. Learn from the mistake

Source: Adapted from Bonoma (1984)

There is some degree of subjectivity when defining appropriate or inappropriate strategies. Strategies are often labelled inappropriate even when they have failed often through poor implementation. Strategies are often labelled appropriate despite being saved by adaptations in implementation or even luck.

Formulating an appropriate strategy has been covered in Section 3.

So what factors are needed for success? These are summarised in Table 12.2.

Table 12.2	Key Strategy Implementation Factors
Key elements of implementation of plans and strategies	
Leadership	Resources
Strategy	Skills
Culture	Systems
Structure	Control

Leadership

The role of the leader is to get the best out of people. Many leaders reach their position based on technical skills which often creates problems. Leaders require effective people skills such as delegation and negotiation and a range of transferable management skills.

The role of leadership is to facilitate activities rather than do the work themselves.

Kotter (1990) suggests that leaders succeed by:

- Establishing direction and strategy
- Communicating it to those whose co-operation is needed
- Motivating and inspiring people

The relative instability and unpredictability of the environment has influenced the emergence of a new concept of leadership, transformational as opposed to transactional leadership. The transformational leader motivates and inspires staff and ensures they understand the vision for the organisation. There is now emphasis on leadership to ensure that the organisation can adapt and succeed in a rapidly changing world.

Kouzes and Posner (2002) outline five characteristics of leadership:

1. Challenging the process – Encourage others to develop ideas and take calculated risks

2. Inspire a shared vision

3. Enabling others to act – Encourage collaboration, co-operation, empowering others

4. Modelling the way – Planning, reviewing progress and taking corrective action

5. Clear about values and acting consistently with them

Leaders need to adopt an appropriate style of management depending on the circumstances.

House (1996) suggests that the appropriate style depends on the characteristics of the subordinates and the work environment (Table 12.3).

Table 12.3	Leadership Styles
Directive style	When task is ambiguous and staff lack flexibility
Supportive style	When tasks are repetitive, frustrating or unpleasant
Achievement orientated style	Non-repetitive, sometimes ambiguous, challenging tasks which need pressure and encouragement to raise performance
Participative style	Non-repetitive and staff are confident in their ability to do the work

Source: Adapted from House (1996)

Strategy

The potential strategy will need to be screened to ensure that it is appropriate to current circumstances. What is the basis of competitive advantage? Does it build on the strengths of the organisation? Are the weaknesses of the organisation addressed? What organisation changes are required to successfully deliver the strategy? How acceptable is the strategy to stakeholders?

Strategy should be an ongoing activity. Throughout the implementation stage, management will need to review and adapt. Strategic objectives should remain the same but changes may be required for the targets to be achieved.

Culture

Culture can be defined as the combination of shared values and beliefs that exist within an organisation. These are commonly observed and reinforced by corporate symbols such as logos. Great care must be exercised when implementing strategy.

A marketing planner or strategist must be sensitive to the shared values that exist within the organisation. A new strategy cannot be successfully executed without developing and maintaining support within the organisation. If the strategy goes against the dominant culture, there is a strong likelihood of failure. Restructuring, internal marketing and staff training will be required if the strategy is to be successfully implemented.

Structure

The structure of the organisation has two primary functions.

1. It defines the lines of authority and levels of responsibility.
2. It provides a basis for communication.

There is a current trend towards flattened structures with more devolved authority and responsibility. It is important to consider how communication occurs, as structures can make senior management remote from customers and impede the flow of information and communication.

Multifunctional teams with a wide range of backgrounds can increase innovation, identify and solve operational problems and improve quality.

Skills

The appropriate skills mix is required to achieve any aim or objective. Successful implementation requires the following:

- Marketing/technical skills – Marketing research, design and R&D

- HRM skills – Selection, training and appraisal
- Project management skills – Forecasting, budgeting, resourcing and monitoring

A range of both hard and soft skills is required. Implementing marketing strategy requires 'soft' human resource management skills as well as the 'hard' project management skills.

Systems

There are two groups of systems required for implementation.

1. Forecasting
2. Reporting

These systems are essential for management decision-making. The marketing information system (MKIS) will be essential for gathering marketing information and marketing decision-making. The management information system (MIS) will cover areas such as finance, operations management, budgeting and monitoring.

Control

This is simply making sure what should happen actually does happen. The basic approach is to monitor and compare with some predetermined standard (a feedback loop) and take action if required. The business plan, the marketing plan, the budget or monthly targets are frequently used as targets.

Resources

A strategic marketing plan must be resourced. Resources usually relate mainly to finance and staff. Resources are normally budget driven, although greater importance is now being given to the importance of time (time to market). Resources are often influenced more by internal politics than needs and the marketing planner should be aware of this influence.

Flexibility is essential and a sensible contingency should be built into the marketing plan to provide a buffer in case things do not go according to plan. Additional resources may be required during the implementation and the success of the strategy may well depend on having access to these, if conditions change.

ORGANISATIONAL STRUCTURES, SYSTEMS AND PROCESSES

Having selected a strategy, the next important step is to select the structure that will deliver the corporate objectives in an efficient and effective way. It is important that the structure and the lines of communication within it are understood by all employees.

The structure of the organisation might be functional, territory or product based.

The functional organisation defines each of the functions with each having a management line of control.

For example, marketing is likely to be headed by a Director of Marketing and control will be exercised through a range of marketing specialisms including sales, market research, new product development and marketing communications. This will allow the marketing team to undertake the day-to-day marketing activities in an integrated way (Figure 12.1).

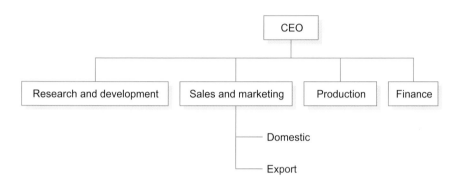

FIGURE 12.1

Functional Organisational Structure

Source: Hollensen (2006)

The advantages of this type of structure are:

- Specialisation leads to efficiency
- Common interests promote good internal relations
- Clear career paths and professional development for employees

The disadvantages of this type of structure are:

- Conflict over priorities
- Isolation from the wider aspects of the organisation

The Geographic or Territory-based Organisation

This is an effective structure where organisations trade regionally or internationally. This is a form of decentralised management. Business management functions, such as resourcing, budgeting and marketing, are devolved to each territory where local management have authority and responsibility to manage but still in line with the corporate goals and objectives.

This approach is typical of large organisations, operating in different regions or countries, especially where cultural differences make decentralised management sensible (Figure 12.2).

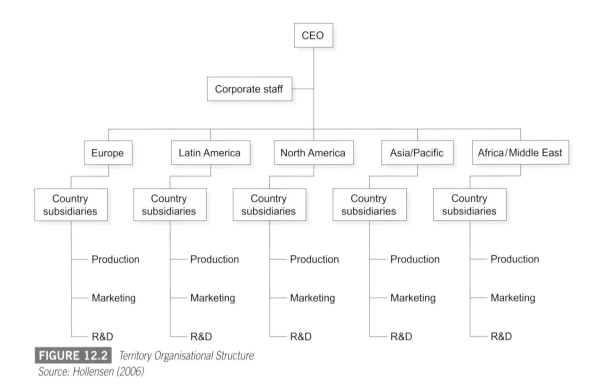

FIGURE 12.2 *Territory Organisational Structure*
Source: Hollensen (2006)

The advantages of this type of structure are:

■ Resources are pooled
■ Co-ordination of different functional areas of management is improved
■ Specialist staff can focus on the region

The disadvantages of this type of structure are:

■ There is a possibility that some products will be overlooked as there is no overall responsibility for specific products
■ Efficiency depends on having a group of highly effective managers

The Product-based Organisation

Major companies such as Philips and Unilever adopt a product-based structure where different brands and products are managed as separate business units.

In a product-based organisation, product managers have devolved responsibility for their particular brand and product and are expected to deliver in line with corporate expectations (Figure 12.3).

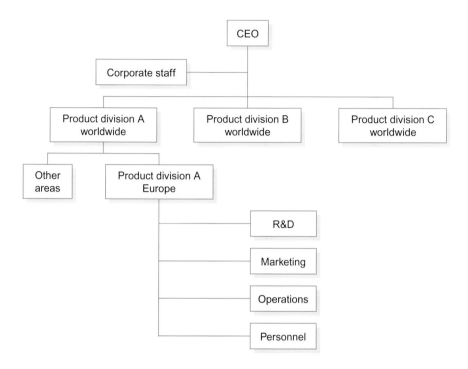

FIGURE 12.3

*Product-Based
Organisational Structure
Source: Hollensen (2006)*

Major advantages of this structure are:

- Decentralisation
- Motivated specialist divisional heads
- Products may be introduced and deleted, without effect on the rest of the organisation

The disadvantages of this structure are:

- Co-ordination problems may arise
- Some products may be overlooked
- Bias when divisional heads move on into corporate management

The Matrix Organisation

Marketing has embraced more and more other business functions in order to develop a more integrated co-ordinated approach to achieve corporate goals. A matrix organisation incorporates many business functions. The real strength of this organisational structure is that it can respond to different political and economic environments because it combines the elements of product-based and territory management. For example, a product manager would have product responsibility worldwide for Product A, whereas geographic managers would be responsibility for all product lines including Product A. The management responsibilities overlap and this provides a good basis for decision-making (Figure 12.4).

The major disadvantages of this structure are:

■ The possibility of power struggles in this dual command structure
■ The structure may collapse in times of crisis
■ Communication can be complicated

The organisational hierarchy determines what decisions people at each level can make. As an organisation grows, the hierarchy becomes more complex. At some point, a decision will need to be made on whether to centralise or to decentralise.

Centralisation: is when those at the top make most decisions, with managers at divisional level responsible for ensuring that the policies are carried out at the operating level.

Decentralisation: is where a relatively large number of decisions are taken in the divisional or operating levels.

A centralised approach provides management at corporate level with more control but decision are usually slow. A decentralised approach to

FIGURE 12.4

*The Matrix Organisational
Structure*

Source: Hollensen (2006)

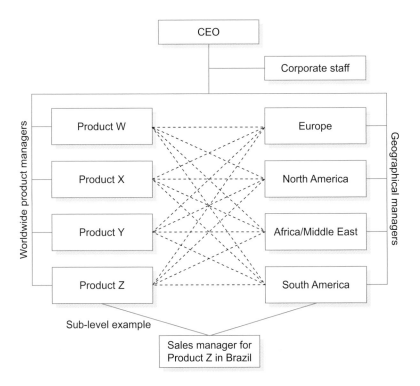

decision-making provides quicker decision-making and decisions are more likely to take account of local conditions.

The structures adopted reflect the history, management outlook and experience of the organisation. Strategy changes will have some effect on the organisation structure. The important thing to remember is the best organisational structure – the one that fits the external environment and the internal characteristics of the organisation.

ACTIVITY 12.1

Select an organisation of your choice. Go to the website of the company and gather information about the structure of the organisation.

Which type of structure has the organisation adopted? What are the benefits of their approach? If the organisation has international operations, how are they represented in the structure? Has the organisation adopted a centralised or decentralised approach?

FORECASTING AND BUDGETING

Forecasting is the process of using available information to develop one or more views of the future. There are a number of techniques which can be used independently or in combination to achieve this. Forecasting is used to provide quantified estimates on which marketing objectives and marketing plans can be based.

Forecasts used in marketing planning usually cover such variables as size of market, market growth, levels of demand for a particular product, rates of adoption or competitors' likely shares of the market.

There are two views of the future.

1. The future will be incrementally the same as the past
2. The future will be radically different from the past

Forecasting techniques can help to provide a view of the future.

FORECASTING TECHNIQUES

There are a number of forecasting techniques available.

Trend Extrapolation

This technique sometimes called time series analysis uses statistical techniques to examine past trends in markets and extrapolate those trends into the future. The technique is based on the view that the future will be incrementally the same as the past. Therefore, this technique is unsuitable for situations where the future is radically different.

Individual Forecasting

An individual, ideally someone considered an expert, predicts events. The individual may come up with an accurate forecast, but this may be a personal judgement and provide a biased view of the world. This can be a high-risk method, therefore consensus forecasting may overcome the weakness.

Consensus Forecasting

This uses a panel of experts who produce a judgement. One method is Jury forecasting – they work together to produce a forecast on which they all agree. However, there is a danger of group think with this approach. Members of the jury may influence each other resulting in an unrealistic forecast. The Delphi forecast attempts to overcome this weakness by using similar experts working independently of each other. It may employ a series of rounds in which each expert gives a view which is then fed back to other experts to be refined. It does not arrive at a single view and consensus is not required. Indeed difference can stimulate new ideas.

Scenario Planning

This is the process of identifying a number of possible futures, instead of a single view of the future. It is usually used by a group of managers who define scenarios which they consider possible. They proceed through a series of set stages to identify relevant variables and critical issues. Models can be built to evaluate scenarios and the question of 'what if?' asked. A plan can then be developed with a range of alternatives considered suitable for the various scenarios.

BUDGETING

> The budget is a financial plan outlined in quantitative terms for a set period, usually a year.

The processes of strategic development and budgeting are connected. The budgeting process translates marketing strategy into financial terms, which are the ways all plans are expressed, evaluated and controlled. A budget is the most common control mechanism and has the following purposes.

- Quantifying the plan
- Co-ordination of activities
- Identifying critical issues
- Assigning responsibility

It should contain estimates for all the functional areas of the organisation. In marketing, this will mean the costs of sales, market research, advertising and other promotional expenditure. The budget is about resource allocation and financial and human resources will be essential for successful implementation. However, the marketing planner should remember budgeting is a political process and negotiation and bargaining will be necessary to obtain the required resources in order to achieve the objectives.

Common approaches to budgeting are:

- Historic – The organisation may simply base the budget on previous financial data making adjustments for factors such as level of activity and inflation.

- Zero-based – These budgets are systematically re-evaluated, examining activities and benefits. Alternative ways of achieving the objectives are considered within the financial constraints.

- Activity-related – These budgets are based measures of activity.

There are a number of different budgeting methods, which is shown in Table 12.4.

While organisations should be customer driven, many organisations are budget driven with objectives related to time and budget.

Marketing planners should remember that budgets can be a key motivational tool with targets being set and rewards being related to the achievement of targets contained in the budget.

Table 12.4	Budgeting Methods
Incremental budgeting	Based on previous year with adjustment for growth and inflation
Objective and task	Budget is based on the estimate of what is needed to achieve the objectives. Clear definition of tasks and resources is necessary
Percentage of sales method	Based on a percentage of the previous years sales being allocated to marketing
Competitive parity	This approach is based on spending the same percentage as others in the industry
Judgement methods	Managers are asked to use their judgement and experience to estimate the marketing costs to achieve different levels of sales
Experiment and test	The organisation may run an experiment in one area to test the effect of advertising to establish the level of advertising required to achieve a specified level of sales

Budgeting is critical for the measuring of the performance of the organisation and individuals. The budget provides the standard for measuring performance. This is achieved by comparing budgeted performance against actual performance (variance analysis).

TIMESCALES AND RESPONSIBILITIES

The marketing planning process begins with the audit of the marketing environment and preparation of the internal analysis. The marketing planning process should be ongoing. The co-ordination of the marketing planning process should be the responsibility of the marketing manager, who should obtain cross-functional support and input to the process.

The marketing function is responsible for identifying customers that the organisation can most effectively satisfy.

An effective MKIS is needed to provide an up-to-date and accurate information. Marketing intelligence and market research will be carried out or co-ordinated by marketing. Information will be gathered on consumer demand, competitor strategies and changes in the marketing environment. Data on its own has no meaning, so it will also be the responsibility of marketing to analyse and extract useful information for marketing and other organisation purposes.

If customer satisfaction is to be achieved, information on changing customer demand, preferences and tastes will need to be distributed throughout the organisation to functions requiring it. Information held by other functions will be useful to ascertain trends, e.g. sales and marketing will be responsible for gathering information. Marketing therefore holds a central position in organisations.

Marketing will be responsible for selecting the most appropriate marketing mix, the media and the messages with which to engage customers in order to achieve the organisational objectives.

Adopting a marketing orientation ensures that the whole organisation is committed to achieving organisational goals by continually satisfying consumer demands. Functional areas need to co-operate and co-ordinate activities towards customer satisfaction. Marketing staff play a key role in encouraging and developing a marketing orientation throughout the organisation. Internal marketing could be used to develop the required cultural changes and this will be the responsibility of marketing.

MANAGERIAL, ORGANISATIONAL AND CULTURAL SHORTCOMINGS

As already noted in Section 1, a range of barriers to effective marketing planning exist. The marketing planner must pay careful attention to these barriers, if marketing plans are to be implemented effectively.

The following are some of the key barriers:

Organisational barriers include:

- Manager's tendency to build empires will cause problems
- A focus on internal politics
- Failure to share information and ideas

Lack of marketing competency within the organisation:

- Insufficient marketing skills
- Poor understanding of the marketing planning process
- Failure to see whole picture – obsession with individual products
- Poor grasp of marketing concept

Lack of management time for effective marketing planning:

- Difficulty balancing day-to-day operations with strategic marketing planning

PLANNING INADEQUACIES

Too Much Short-term Marketing

- Too much emphasis on a one-year time frame.
- No long-term vision

Marketing Plans Developed in Isolation Rather than on Marketing Analysis

- Lack of marketing intelligence system
- Poor sharing of marketing intelligence
- Insufficient analysis of competitors
- Poor understanding of the environment
- Insufficient understanding of customer behaviour

FAILURE TO INTEGRATE INTO CORPORATE PLANNING SYSTEM

In many organisations, whilst marketing plans may be prepared, the marketing planning process is not integrated across the organisation, possible reasons are as follows.

Isolation of Marketing Planning from Other Business Areas

- Lack of involvement by different functional areas
- Lack of enthusiasm from non-marketing areas
- Limited power of marketers to co-ordinate different functional areas in process

McDonald (2007) suggests a range of barriers to the implementation of strategic marketing planning.

Barriers to the Implementation of Marketing Planning

1. Weak support from the chief executive and top management
2. Lack of a plan for planning
3. Lack of line management support
4. Confusion over planning terms
5. Numbers in place of written objectives and strategies
6. Too much detail, too far ahead
7. Once-a-year ritual
8. Separation of operational planning from strategic planning
9. Delegation to a planner
10. Failure to integrate marketing planning into total planning system

In many organisations, the marketing plan or budget is simply an annual chore, something to do and get over as quickly as possible, rather than a meaningful and critical strategic process.

MONITORING AND CONTROL MECHANISMS

Monitoring and control is essential if the marketing plan is to be successfully executed. We need to monitor to ensure things are going according to plan and take corrective action if they are not.

Marketers are increasingly being pressurised by senior management to become more accountable for their activities and expenditure and are expected to monitor, control and evaluate activities.

Monitoring and control has four key elements:

1. Objective setting
2. Setting performance standards
3. Monitoring and evaluation of performance
4. Reaction – Taking corrective action as required

Monitoring and control involves setting standards, measurement, evaluation and monitoring, and aims to translate strategic plans into specific actions. They may include: financial measures, budgets, performance appraisal and benchmarking. These should be used to highlight where corrective action is necessary.

Effective monitoring and control systems should be flexible and should have the following attributes.

- Involvement – Staff are encouraged to participate (particularly relevant for a service organisation)

- Target setting should be quantifiable and achievable and be communicated in advance

- Recognise problems and not just symptoms

- Measure effectiveness and not just efficiency

- Management by exception – Take corrective action only if results fall outside tolerance zones (concentrate on the important issues)

- Should promote action – Not just detect problems

Budgetary control involves financial control of the whole business through a system of budgets. There will be a master budget for the whole organisation, together with subsidiary budgets for each of the functions of the organisation, marketing, HR, etc. There will also be a cash budget to identify the cash implications of the various functional budgets and a capital budget for the major items of expenditure, such as new machinery.

Resources are scarce and costly, so it is important to have controls and measurements clearly identified in marketing plans. A marketing manager will be expected to compare actual figures against predetermined standards set out in the budget. Corrective action, if required, can then be taken and an investigation undertaken to establish precisely why the difference or variance has occurred.

Variance Analysis

Variance analysis is used as part of the budgetary control process to identify movements of actual performance away from budget. The objective is to identify variances from budget on a regular basis (monthly) so that corrective action can be taken.

A typical layout for a monthly or annual budget report is shown in Table 12.5.

Control systems need to be carefully designed. No system is perfect and no system is 100% accurate. There are three problems of control systems, which must be remembered:

1. They are costly – So the costs should not outweigh the benefits

2. They stifle effort and creativity – The motivational effects need to be considered

3. They promote attitudes of inspection – The focus on symptoms rather than problems

Table 12.5	Annual Budget Report			
	Budgeted	**Actual**	**Variance under**	**Variance over**
Sales	5,000	5,200		+200
Direct labour	2,000	2,200		+200
Direct materials	1,000	1,050		+50
Royalties	500	450	−50	
License fees	100	50	−50	
Contribution	1,400	1,250		
Overheads	1,000	1,000		
Net income	400	250		

Care must be taken to avoid extensive bureaucratic systems which will often consume resources and take the focus away from the customer.

Benchmarking

> A systematic and ongoing process of measuring and comparing an organisation's business processes and achievements against acknowledged process leaders and/or key competitors to facilitate improved performance.

Benchmarking is about the pursuit of continuous improvement. An organisation using benchmarking shows it is a learning organisation, willing to learn from mistakes and seeking to develop best practice.

There are three elements.

Competitor analysis: Reviewing competitors' activities and identifying areas where the organisation can improve.

Best Practice: Investigating and analysing the best way to carry out activities. This may require going outside the industry to take a more innovative approach.

Performance standards: Many industries publish industry standards, which can be used to compare an individual organisations performance.

The whole process is about adaptation, identifying ideas and practices and adapting for the organisation. Typical areas that are bench marked are customer service levels, logistics and time to market.

PERFORMANCE METRICS

The objectives set by the organisation need to be supported by appropriate measures that can be used continuously to monitor performance against those objectives. Traditionally, measures have been financial, with the accountancy profession dominating the debate on how to measure performance.

Marketing does not have standardised techniques for measuring performance, consequently marketing expenditure and budgets may be allocated in an arbitrary way.

The performance measures selected have a strong influence on the behaviour of both management and employees. The measures selected will have an influence on what actually gets done.

Financial performance is measured in terms of return on investment or profitability. Gross profit measures the profit margin and reflects changes in prices and costs. Intense competition may result in lower prices and a reduction in margin. The net profit, often referred to as the bottom line, will be influenced by the gross profit margin and the overheads of the organisation. Measures such as return on capital employed and return on investment relate the profitability of the organisation to the financial resources employed to achieve that profit.

PROFITABILITY AND RETURN MEASURES

(a) Gross margin $\dfrac{\text{Gross profit}}{\text{Sales revenue}} \times 100$

(b) Net margin $\dfrac{\text{Net profit}}{\text{Sales revenue}} \times 100$

(c) Return on capital employed (ROCE) $\dfrac{\text{Net profit}}{\text{Capital employed}} \times 100$
(where capital employed = total assets less current liliabilities)

Although profitability is important, it is important to measure the long-term stability of the organisation. Those organisations will heavy borrowings carry a greater risk of failure than those with lower levels of debt. Those with higher levels of borrowing will find it harder to maintain interest payments and meet the terms of the finance when the economic environment is difficult.

LONG-TERM SOLVENCY AND STABILITY MEASURES

(a) Debt ratio $\dfrac{\text{Total debt}}{\text{Total assets}}$

(b) Capital gearing $\dfrac{\text{Long-term debt}}{\text{Total capital employed}}$

(c) Debt/equity ratio $\dfrac{\text{Debt}}{\text{Ordinary share capital and reserves}}$

(d) Interest cover $\dfrac{\text{Profit before interest and tax (PBIT)}}{\text{Interest charges}}$

(e) Cash flow ratio $\dfrac{\text{Net cash inflow}}{\text{Total debts}}$

The ability to meet short-term liabilities is crucial to survival. Profitable businesses have failed where they have inadequate working capital or facilities in place and they have been unable to meet financial claims on time. Solvency and liquidity ratios are used to measure the ability to meet these short-term claims.

SHORT-TERM SOLVENCY AND LIQUIDITY MEASURES

(a) Current ratio $\dfrac{\text{Current assets}}{\text{Current liabilities}}$

(b) Quick ratio $\dfrac{\text{Current assets less stocks}}{\text{Current liabilities}}$

Various financial ratios are used to measure the efficiency of the organisation. How quickly does stock turnover? How long is stock left unsold? How quickly are payments from customers collected?

EFFICIENCY MEASURES

(a) Stock turnover $\dfrac{\text{Cost of sales}}{\text{Stock}}$ or $\dfrac{\text{Stock}}{\text{Cost of sales}} \times 365$

(b) Debtors' turnover $\dfrac{\text{Credit sales}}{\text{Trade debtors}}$ or $\dfrac{\text{Trade debtors}}{\text{Credit sales}} \times 365$

(c) Creditors' turnover $\dfrac{\text{Purchases}}{\text{Trade creditors}}$ or $\dfrac{\text{Trade creditors}}{\text{Purchases}} \times 365$

It is now becoming increasingly important for marketers to develop and use measures (metrics) that will measure the effectiveness of marketing alongside the traditional financial measures shown above. These metrics of brand equity, customer satisfaction, loyalty and retention and share of voice have been gradually adopted. However, many organisations still rely on the traditional financial measures.

There are three main areas that performance measures should cover:

1. Efficiency
2. Effectiveness
3. Innovation or adaptability

The efficiency measures in marketing show the ability of the organisation to utilise its asset base. Efficiency can be described as the ratio of outputs achieved compared to the inputs. Efficiency will mean different things to different organisations but typical metrics used are given in Table 12.6.

Table 12.6	Efficiency Metrics
Efficiency	
Capacity utilisation	Inventory levels
Sales turnover per employee	Conversion of enquiries to sales
Speed of delivery	

Efficiency is not enough. Every organisation needs to assess the effectiveness of its marketing strategies. Effectiveness measures the extent to which organisational goals and objectives are achieved – 'are we doing the right things'. The performance measures selected will vary from organisation to organisation and from industry to industry. Some of the typical measures used are given in Table 12.7.

Table 12.7	Effectiveness Metrics
Effectiveness	
Number of customers	Number of new customers
Unit sales	Customer loyalty
Market share by volume	Customer complaints
Market share by segment	Customer loyalty
Relative value	Relative quality

If an organisation is to be successful, it will have to adapt to the changing environment. Innovation and adaptation will need to be high on the agenda. Typical metrics which are used to measure innovation are given in Table 12.8.

Metrics can also be used to measure brand equity (Table 12.9).

Table 12.8	Innovation Metrics
Innovation	
Number of patents registered	New product success rates
Trade marks registered	Number of R& D projects
Percentage of sales from new products/ services	Acquisition/introduction of new brands

Table 12.9	Brand Equity Metrics
Brand equity	
Purchase intent	Brand value
Customer preference	Brand strength
Brand value	Level of trust in the brand

The increase in online and digital marketing has led to the development of another range of performance metrics, which are given in Table 12.10.

Table 12.10	Online Performance Metrics
Online performance tracking	
Click-through rates	The number of times that users click on advertisement
Cost per click	The amount spent by the advertiser to generate one click through
Cost per lead	The amount spent by the advertiser to generate one lead
Cost per sale	The amount spent by the advertiser to generate one sale

Competitive conditions and the changing environment will require a combination of performance measures. The triple bottom line (TBL) approach uses a range of measures, social, environmental and financial to judge success in the market place. The TBL is considered an approach which will provide a more balanced view of the overall performance of an organisation.

ACTIVITY 12.2

Select an organisation that you are familiar with.

Using the above framework of measures, select a range of metrics that would cover the financial, social and environmental performance of the organisation.

When selecting performance measures the following should be considered:

- Is the measure suitable for the required purpose?
- Is the measure acceptable to key functions and stakeholders?
- Is it feasible, given resource constraints?
- Can the measure be used for benchmarking?

Financial measures will continue to be important because of reporting requirements. However, it is likely that marketing measures will become increasingly important for determining organisational performance and strategic, environmental and ethical health.

CONTINGENCY PLANNING

Events in the real world rarely go according to plan. It is therefore essential that those preparing marketing plans consider the problems that might occur and make appropriate preparations to deal with them should the need arise.

Contingency planning is the opportunity to recognise different scenarios or series of events and to develop plans that involve different activities being taken at different times. The organisation must develop a capacity to adapt to new circumstances.

The organisation will need to set aside financial reserves and specific resources such as productive capacity.

Consideration should be given to developing contingencies covering a variety of scenarios such as the loss of a major contract, the loss of productive capacity through fire or flood, or delays in time to market.

Contingency planning should ensure that there is a prompt response to difficulties or delays in implementation or any unexpected events. Many organisations incorporate a contingency figure into the budget (say 5 or 10%)

INTERNAL MARKETING

> Internal marketing is the application of marketing internally within the organisation, with programmes of communication and guidance targeted at internal audiences to develop responsiveness and a unified sense of purpose among employees.
>
> Dibb et al. (2006)

The implementation of a new corporate strategy may also require change within the organisation and the internal marketing plan will play a critical role in obtaining 'buy in' and a positive reaction from employees.

Marketing orientation can only be achieved when everybody in the organisation is customer focussed (both internal and external customers). Internal marketing again plays a fundamental role in helping to achieve this.

A number of internal cultural barriers may exist that can inhibit the development of a market led orientation. These are:

- Fear of change
- Lack of time
- Poor communication
- Lack of understanding
- A cynical view of marketing

Internal marketing is an approach that can be used to overcome these barriers. Internal marketing covers any planned effort to overcome resistance in an organisation to change and to ensure proper communication, motivation and training employees effectively to implement corporate and functional strategies and plans.

Internal marketing focusses on the relationship between the organisation and its employees. Berry and Parasuraman (1991) define the process in terms of viewing employees (or groups of employees) as internal customers.

Successful implementation is reliant on three key skills:

1. Persuasion

   - Present a shared vision
   - Sell the benefits
   - Communicate and train
   - Eliminate misconceptions
   - Gain acceptance by association
   - Support words with clear actions

2. Negotiation

   - Make the opening proposition high – allow room for negotiation
   - Trade concessions with different parties

3. Politics

   - Building coalitions
   - Take incremental steps
   - Invite the opposition in
   - Control the agenda

The internal marketing plan provides a framework as follows:

- Vision, aims and objectives
- Internal marketing strategy

- Segmentation, targeting and positioning
- Marketing mix programme
- Implementation
- Monitoring and control

Segmentation

Segmentation is the process of dividing groups into subgroups that have similar characteristics. Staff may be segmented by function, status, full-time/part-time or other segmentation variable.

An alternative approach is to segment according to the support for the strategy, as shown in Table 12.11.

Table 12.11 Segmenting Internal Markets		
Segment 1	**Segment 2**	**Segment 3**
Influential supporter	Influential opposition	Non-involved supporter

Each group have different concerns and may require different training needs from other staff groups delivered through the internal marketing mix.

Product

This is likely to be the process of change or the new strategy. It is useful to think of the job of each individual as an internal product, essential in delivering the overall strategy.

Promotion

Communication is a key component of internal marketing. There needs to be a promotional campaign stressing the benefits of the change or new strategy. Discussion groups, presentations, and newsletters, for example, could all be used to achieve awareness and get the change message across.

Place (or distribution)

How is the 'product' going to be delivered to the internal customer? Meetings, team briefings, seminars, magazine, notice boards and the intranet will be used.

Price

This is a complex area. The costs of change and the cost of the communications can be calculated easily. However, the psychological cost of uncertainty and stress will be carried by the staff. These costs such as loss of status, change in work pattern, a change in income are costs that internal customers must pay as a result of accepting the plan.

QUESTIONS

1. Why are marketing measures now considered to be an important aspect of a company's performance?

2. What are the barriers to the implementation of an internal marketing programme?

SUMMARY

This chapter has considered the key elements of implementation within the marketing planning process. These are critical to its ultimate success or failure. The preparation and delivery of marketing plans and new strategies will require appropriate structures and resources. Forecasting and budgeting, timings and responsibilities all need to be carefully determined to ensure that implementation is effective, and there are sometimes shortcomings in these areas. Measures will be required to monitor, control and assess the way in which the organisation performs against the targets set out in the plan. Internal marketing will be critical for communicating the changes required for the delivery of the strategy throughout the organisation, and in addressing the barriers that may exist that inhibit uptake of the plan.

BIBLIOGRAPHY

Berry, L. and Parasuraman, A. (1991) *Marketing Services: Competing Through Quality*. Free Press, New York.

Bonoma, T. (1984) Making Your Marketing Strategies Work. *Harvard Business Review*, 62(2), 69–76.

Dibb, S., Simkin, L., Pride, W. and Ferrell, O.C. (2006) *Marketing: Concepts and Strategies*, 5th edition. Houghton Mifflin, Boston.

Hollensen, S. (2006) *Marketing Planning, A Global Perspective*. McGraw Hill, London.

House, R.J. (1996) Path-Goal Theory of Leadership: Lessons, Legacy and a Reformulation. *Leadership Quarterly*, 7(3), 323–352.

Kotter, J.P. (1990) *A Force for Change: How Leadership Differs from Management*. Free Press, New York.

Kouzes, J. and Posner, B. (2002) *The Leadership Challenge*, 3rd edition. Jossey-Bass, San Francisco.

McDonald, M. (2007) *Marketing Plans How to Prepare Them, How to Use Them*, 6th edition. Butterworth Heinemann, Oxford.

Piercy, N. (2002) *Market Led Strategic Change*, 3rd edition. Butterworth Heinemann, Oxford.

CHAPTER 13

Approaches to Implementing the Process of Marketing Planning

LEARNING OBJECTIVES

4.3   Propose and justify approaches to implementing the process of marketing planning in different contextual settings

SYLLABUS REFERENCES

4.3:

- marketing planning for different stakeholder groups
- planning in consumer and B2B markets
- services marketing planning
- issues of marketing planning in large and small organisations
- internal marketing segmentation
- marketing planning in non-profit organisations
- the international and global dimension of marketing planning
- marketing planning in highly competitive markets
- facilitating relationship-based marketing planning and customer retention
- planning marketing in the virtual marketplace

INTRODUCTION

This chapter looks at marketing planning and the implementation of marketing plans in a range of different contexts. Marketing planning is commonly associated with large FMCG organisations, with strong brands and large budgets. The process of marketing planning and the benefits from it are applicable to a wide range of organisations whether domestic or international, large or small and for profit or the not for profit.

In this section, we will explore marketing planning for the following.

- Fast moving consumer goods (FMCG)
- B2B goods and services
- Services
- Small and medium-sized enterprises (SMEs)
- Not-for-profit organisations
- International and global enterprises
- Marketing planning in the virtual market place

MARKETING PLANNING FOR FMCG

The FMCG market is particularly competitive. In the UK, a FMCG company developing a new brand will be selling not only in the domestic markets but also across Europe and much of the world. Therefore, there must be a more global vision in the development of new products and brand strategies.

Consistent quality will be important for success and the brand name can be critical. Considerable financial resources will be essential, since establishing a brand may take several years and require a heavy expenditure on product development as well as marketing communications.

FMCG packaged goods organisations must take a multilingual approach or a non-verbal approach or must be prepared for the high expenditure of packaging products in a number of different languages. The FMCG market is particularly competitive with major players fighting for market share, therefore appropriate products and brand strategies are required.

FMCG organisations selling packaged goods must consider whether they are going to use product names and brand names and whether they should be used independently or combined.

Where there is a relationship between product and brand names, marketing can develop an integrated approach with marketing communication messages developing associations between product and brand. Messages that are related to quality help to reduce price sensitivity and develop a competitive position.

Where there are successful products and strong brand associations, organisations will find it easier to introduce new products or extend existing product lines. However, there are also many benefits associated with keeping products and brands separate.

- Provides greater flexibility for packaging and promotions.
- When an organisation is test marketing a new product, there is less risk of being damaged by the failure of that product.
- The failure of a product will be less likely to damage the brand.

The success of any FMCG product is based on the success of a well planned and integrated marketing mix. The product and the brand play an important part, but we should not forget the other elements of the marketing mix and how they contribute to the success of FMCG organisations.

The Marketing Mix for FMCG Organisations

Place

In terms of place, an organisation must consider whether its strategy will be:

- Intensive
- Selective
- Exclusive

FMCG organisations will mostly adopt an intensive distribution strategy. This means that the products will be widely available and will be seen in many outlets. Chocolate bars are found in supermarkets, petrol stations, newsagents, leisure centres, DIY stores and garden centres, and at airports and railway stations. Ice cream, soft drinks and paper tissues are further examples of products where an intensive distribution strategy has been adopted.

Intensive distribution is based on the idea that market coverage is more important than the types of stores selling the product. The expansion of the range of goods sold by DIY stores and garden centres illustrates the intensive distribution strategies adopted by major confectionery, ice-cream and clothing companies.

Price

Pricing in the FMCG sector is a very difficult element to manage as a consequence of the intense competition in these markets. Major FMCG organisations are constantly striving to attain an increased market share. Price skimming is less likely to be found in these markets than others you will be studying. FMCG organisations are highly responsive to market demands and consumer needs in terms of price, but also need to take account of brand positioning.

Promotion

The most common communications used by FMCGs are advertising and sales promotion. High levels of expenditure are made by FMCG organisations on marketing communications each year.

In the FMCG markets, the main elements of the marketing communications mix are:

- Packaging
- Point of purchase

- Merchandising
- Direct mail (competitions and money off coupons)
- Websites
- Advertising
- Sponsorship
- Corporate identity
- Public relations
- Product placement
- Trade promotions

FMCG organisations use a variety of tools to communicate and develop their brands with retailers, customers and other stakeholders. The aim is to introduce the organisation and their brands to their audiences and to engage with them, stimulating them to make a succession of purchases over the long term. These organisations use a variety of media and messages some being informational and some emotional to engage with their audiences.

Major FMCG organisation such as Proctor and Gamble, Unilever and Cadbury have developed thought provoking and entertaining television advertisements to engage with their audience. In December 2008, Unilever ran an advertisement for PG tips, the Monkey's Christmas speech. Cadbury ran a campaign in 2007 with a Gorilla playing the drums which became a very successful viral campaign.

This is a market characterised by price and non-price competition and constant promotional battles. Common sights are 'Buy one, get one free', 'Three for the price of two', 'Extra 10% free' and 'Extra reward points'.

A major development has been the introduction of rewards schemes operated by the major supermarkets to develop customer loyalty and repeat purchases.

ACTIVITY 13.1

Select a FMCG company of your choice. How does this company use marketing communications to engage with its audience? You will find some of the FMCG websites have examples of previous award winning campaigns.

MARKETING PLANNING IN B2B MARKETS

Marketing in B2B markets presents a range of different challenges to those to be found in B2C markets. It is therefore useful to understand the differences between these two market types (Table 13.1).

There are various terms used to describe B2B markets; a frequently used one is organisational markets and marketing within this context is often termed industrial marketing.

Table 13.1	Major differences between B2B and B2C Markets	
Characteristic	**B2C**	**B2B**
Nature of demand	Primary demand	Derived or joint demand
Nature of buyer	Purchase by individual/ family	Group decision
Seller emphasis	Immediate satisfaction	Economic needs
Customer needs	Groups with similar needs	Each customer has different needs
Purchase motivation	Individual or family need	Multiple buying influences
		Support company operations
Time effects	Short-term relationship	Long-term relationship
Products	Lower technical detail	Technically sophisticated
Price decisions	Price generally fixed. Discounts important	Price determined before purchase. Terms important
Place decisions	Large numbers of small buyers	Limited number of large buyers
Customer service	Less important	Critical for success
Legal factors	Contracts only on major purchases	Contractual arrangements
Environmental arrangements	Impact on demand is direct	Sales impact both directly and indirectly through derived demand

An organisational market is where buyers within an organisation buy on behalf of the organisations they work for. Typical products handled in these organisational markets are, plant and machinery, computers, raw materials, components and stationery.

Organisational markets include manufacturers, hospitals, hotels, wholesalers, retailers as well government departments.

B2B or organisational buying behaviour is influenced by a range of factors:

- The buying situation
- The size and volume of the purchase
- The amount of money available
- The level of risk
- The time frame for decisions
- The purpose of the purchase
- Competitive offers
- Credit terms and conditions of purchase
- Delivery lead times

One of the most important factors the marketing planner must take into account is derived demand. The demand in B2B markets will be derived from the demand in consumer markets. Increases in demand for consumer products will be followed by demand for capital goods, to produce more consumer goods (plant and machinery for instance) and increased demand for materials and components. For example, demand for electrical components such as microchips will be determined by demand for end-user products such as computers, mobile phones and MP3 players.

ACTIVITY 13.2

Select a product, e.g. a car and consider what items would be sourced through organisational markets. For the same product, explain how the demand for these items is dependent upon the demand for the product in its end-user markets.

A downturn in economic activity, such as the 2009 recession, will have a big impact on organisational markets where demand in that market depends on the demand in other markets.

Organisational buying behaviour is influenced by a wide range of factors which are presented below:

- Finance available
- Purpose of the purchase
- The size and volume of purchase
- The buying situation
- The level of risk
- Delivery lead times
- Supply and demand
- Competitive offerings
- The time frame for decision-making
- Organisational objectives
- Conditions of purchase
- Credit terms
- Contract terms
- Demand inelasticities
- Individual relationships
- Environmental factors
- Packaging
- PESTLE factors

The objectives and motivations of buyers in organisational markets are going to be very different from typical buyers in consumer markets.

Their function and objectives will revolve around the organisation and its customers.

These buyers are better informed, more technically minded, more rational and generally more demanding than typical consumer purchasers.

However, marketing planners should be aware that sometimes they have their own personal goals and agendas.

The organisational buyer will be most frequently interested in the overall value proposition because they are responsible for obtaining the best deals for the organisation. The key considerations in relation to the value proposition are quality, delivery, service, the range of products available and price.

You should expect the buyer to demand significant amounts of information, technical specifications and performance specifications and require access to a range of staff for advice before they will make an (informed) decision. They will also have researched the competition and will be aware of other options, prices and alternatives.

The Buying and Decision-making Process in Organisational Markets

The organisational markets have a decision-making unit or buying centre. The roles of a typical decision-making unit for the organisational markets is shown in Table 13.2.

Decisions can have far-reaching consequences, which will have implications for years to come. History and previous experience of the organisation will be a key influence on the choice of supplier in B2B markets.

There are two approaches to managing suppliers as indicated in Table 13.3.

The approach adopted tends to reflect a number of factors such as market structure and, in particular, the culture and objectives of the businesses involved.

Table 13.2	The Decision-Making Unit (Buying Centre)
User	The person who actually uses the product
Influencer	Typical influencers will be users, R&D staff accountants
Decider	Individual buyer, management team, tendering committee
Buyer	The person who will handle the sourcing, information seeking and negotiations
Gatekeeper	Usually secretarial and administrative staff who handle the flow of information through the organisation

Table 13.3	Approaches to Managing Suppliers	
Adversarial	**Collaborative**
Multiple suppliers	Few suppliers
Regular price quotations given	Long-term relationships
Little co-operation	Partnerships
Infrequent use of marketing communications	Frequent use of marketing communications
Ad hoc approach to operations	Integrated approach to operations
Quality	Quality designed in
Emphasis on lowest price	Emphasis on the value proposition

Market Segmentation

Segmentation will help to serve to specific markets more thoroughly and is as important in organisational markets as consumer markets.

Segmentation criteria will include:

- Type of industry
- Size of company
- Type of product or service
- Type of buyer
- Location

In order to target customers, it will be useful to know the people involved in the buying process and the nature of the benefits they are seeking.

The Marketing Mix for Organisational Markets

Product

The type of product will be wide ranging and can involve complex technical specifications (e.g. customised machinery) or alternatively simple raw materials such as screws and nails. The nature of the product depends on what the customer wants, which will affect buying behaviour and aspects of how it is provided such as service – which we will explore later.

Place

There is likely to be a wide distributor network similar to the wholesaler to retailer network found in consumer markets. These need to be incentivised and supported.

Price

Pricing will be based on a variety of methods and will be subject to negotiations and sometimes tenders. Reliability of supply is a key component and, therefore, switching of suppliers is less likely than in consumer markets.

Promotion

Promotion in B2B markets is very different to promoting consumer products, whilst advertising will be necessary, more emphasis will be paced on direct marketing and personal selling backed up with sales literature.

MARKETING PLANNING FOR SERVICES

There are major differences between the marketing of goods and the marketing of services. However, there is one common factor; consumers purchase goods and services for the benefits that each provides.

Marketing planners are faced with a variety of challenges relating to the characteristics of services, the gap between expectations and what is delivered, and the different views on what constitutes a quality service.

The UK and European service sector is growing rapidly. In the UK, over two-thirds of the workforce is engaged in the tertiary sector working in a wide range of service jobs. An economic slow down, such as the current recession of 2009, will slow the growth of services but in the long term the sector is expected to grow further.

One of the main reasons for the growth of the services sector is the changing lifestyles of the population. Economic growth has created the demand for more services and consumers spend more on financial services, travel and leisure services than ever before. People may enjoy a standard of living greater than previous generations but they are time poor. Therefore, more people are buying services such as takeaway meals, landscape gardening, home maintenance and cleaning in order to provide quality time with their families. Changes in society have led to changes in lifestyles and new services have emerged to fulfil all sorts of new needs.

In order to successfully deliver any form of service, it is important to understand what implementation means in practice.

An intangible product involving a deed, a performance or an effort that cannot be physically possessed.

Dibb et al. (2006)

Table 13.4	Consumer and Business Services
Consumer services	Financial services Professional services Personal services, e.g. Hairdressing Education Health Leisure Tourism
Business services	Accountancy Advertising Market research Banking Consultancy services Transport Recruitment services

Services are usually divided into two main sectors, consumer services and business services as shown in Table 13.4.

Consumer services can be provided by both non-profit-making organisations (health, education, charities and the government) and by profit-making organisations (insurance, banking, entertainment and hairdressing).

Whether customers buy goods or services, they purchase for the benefits each provides. However, there are differences between goods and services which the marketing planner must be aware of. Services have five main characteristics:

1. Intangibility
2. Inseparability of production and consumption
3. Perishability
4. Heterogeneity
5. Lack of ownership

Let us examine each of these characteristics in turn.

Intangibility

Services are intangible because there is no physical product. There is no physical substance, nothing to see, touch, taste or smell before purchase. Customers are therefore, unable to understand, imagine or perceive what the service is going to be like.

The major challenge for a service provider is to ensure that the service is analysed and the extent of the intangible elements assessed. Tangible elements can then be added to aid the understanding and expectations of the customer. Insurance organisations offer insurance; therefore, they are covering potential losses, providing security and peace of mind. To overcome the intangibility of this service, they provide quality documentation.

A key characteristic of intangibility is that one the service has been provided, it cannot be used again. Services are provided on one occasion only. The service provided at the supermarket check out, at the bank or by a driving instructor will never be delivered in exactly the same way twice.

Inseparability

An important distinction, exists between products bought and used many times by a customer and services which as consumed as they are purchased. For instance: having a haircut means it is not possible for anyone else to have the same haircut and stylist at the same time.

Inseparability has important implications for the service provider. The involvement of the customer in the production and the delivery service means that the service provider must take great care in what is being provided.

Perishability

Services are perishable because they are produced and consumed at the same time. Goods can be produced and stored to be used later or sold later. Services cannot be stored and consumed at a later date.

For example, if you consider an aircraft flight, if you do not take up your seat and it is not booked by anyone else, it cannot be used again. That flight has gone for ever.

Perishability and fluctuations in demand can affect the sales revenue and profitability of organisations. The airline seat not taken, the hotel room empty, the dental appointment not kept all represent time past and revenue lost.

Organisations have responded to this problem in different ways. In health care, missed dental appointments may be charged for. Last minute discount deals for holidays, hotel rooms and airline flights have become available as more organisations attempt to get some revenue rather than none in these circumstances.

Heterogeneity

Sometimes referred to as variability, heterogeneity means that the service is different. The service can be provided several thousand times, but each time there will be variances in the service delivery. It is highly unlikely customers will ever receive exactly the same service delivery and quality twice. A service cannot be produced, quality assured and boxed like products. It is extremely difficult to determine the quality and level of service because services are produced as they are consumed.

This is a major challenge in the marketing of business services. There is no guarantee the service will be as marketed because of the variability of human nature and behaviour or simply human error.

Lack of Ownership

Services do not result in the transfer of ownership. When we use the services of a rail company, we are transported from one place to another but no transfer of ownership takes place. On arriving at our destination, the only evidence of the service may be part of our ticket. This lack of ownership is a characteristic of many services such as banking, insurance, air travel and medical care. However, retailing is a service and in this case, ownership of tangible goods is transferred. The lack of ownership and the intangible nature of services may lessen the perceived value of a service. The provision of symbolic tangible items are often provided to overcome the problem. Examples would be theatre programmes and quality folders for insurance policies.

According to Mudie and Cottam (1999), service organisations need to understand and recognise the importance of the first law of services, which states:

$$\text{Satisfaction} = \text{Perception} - \text{Expectation}$$

In services marketing, we need to understand the behaviour and perceptions before and after the event. This is essential to ascertain whether the service exceeds, equals or fails to meet expectations. However, as individual perceptions and interpretations will differ, the result of using the above formula can be quite subjective. Yet, measuring customer perceptions is essential for adopting the correct marketing mix and pursuing continuous improvement in services.

The Service Marketing Mix

The marketer has the traditional elements of the marketing mix, referred to as the 4Ps, available. These are product, price, place and promotion. To these we can add a further 3Ps, physical evidence, people and processes. It is these last three elements of the services marketing mix that gives the opportunity to establish a high-quality service.

Physical Evidence – The Physical Environment

The physical evidence element of the marketing mix relates to the place where the services are prepared and or delivered. In the example of a restaurant service, the actual restaurant where the meal is both delivered and consumed will be the physical environment.

When establishing the marketing mix for services, the physical environment will play a major role in establishing the quality perception of the service and the organisation.

The physical environment can be portrayed, through staff uniforms, interior design and relaxing surroundings. Well-known brands such as Harvester and David Lloyd Leisure have made significant investment in high quality surroundings to convey consistency and guaranteed service in support of the brand.

People

One of the big challenges in planning the service marketing mix is the element of human nature. The people element is seen as critical to the delivery of a quality service with good customer care.

Managing the people element of the marketing mix requires strong interpersonal skills, leadership, team management, training and an effective internal marketing programme. The role of staff, their contribution and value to the service process needs to be communicated. The people aspect of the mix should include the following:

- Professional recruitment – Search for attitude, then train for skills
- Investing in staff and training – Organisational training as well as product/service
- Empowerment of staff – Staff to make a full contribution
- Internal marketing – Communications with and motivating staff
- Authority to make decisions – Ability to make fast decisions related to service delivery

Process

Process is about developing ways of delivering the service that will add value to the customer experience. It is important for organisations to develop systems that allow service providers to provide a seamless passage through the customer service experience.

Processes will be essential to the customer experience, but they should be discrete or invisible. The customer requires the whole experience to be a positive one. The processes should be managed with the customers in mind. What are their expectations, their needs and wants? Processes should be designed to deliver all elements of the service to the customer with the minimum of trouble or delay.

The process of booking a holiday or a flight will involve a considerable number of stages from advice, through the booking, payment and finally to receipt of tickets. Every step must be considered and viewed from the customer experience.

ACTIVITY 13.3

Select a service organisation of your choice. Identify and illustrate the importance of each of the extended mix elements, physical evidence, people and processes in the effective delivery of that service to its customers.

The Marketing Mix for Services

Product

The lack of tangibility poses a challenge to the marketing planner. Think benefits; stress the psychological rather than the physical aspects.

Price

Price might be set according to demand, for example, rail and electricity prices reflect differences in demand and varying off peak charges are set.

The price charged for a service will frequently be based around the service value proposition, with some influence from the proportion of intangibility and market forces.

The marketing planner should remember that price will provide a perception of quality.

Place

Physical evidence can play an important part in the case of place. Restaurants, leisure facilities and clubs are examples where physical evidence plays a major part.

Services might deliver to the customer, e.g. Ocado, the home delivery service of grocery retailers Waitrose.

The element of place has changed rapidly with the growth of the Internet with many services being of a virtual nature. Here, the physical evidence will be provided by the quality of the customer experience in the use of the website.

Promotion

The greater the level of intangibility, the more difficult it is to promote.

Positioning, with its relationship with core values will need to be carefully considered when planning the promotional activities.

'Don't promise what you cannot deliver'

Key Components of Designing a Services Mix

In addition to the importance of the 7Ps of the services marketing mix, we should consider the design elements of the service mix.

Mudie and Cottam (1999) suggested service design principles should be considered, which are shown in Table 13.5.

People, physical evidence and processes are critical to the delivery of exceptional service quality.

It will always be difficult for a service organisation to deliver 100% quality. However, service organisations should always consider:

- Customers' expectations
- Service specifications
- Employee performance
- Managing customer service expectations

The SERVQUAL (Parasuraman et al., 1985) model can be used to measure quality within the service sector. It looks at five key factors:

1. Reliability – The ability to perform the service dependably and accurately
2. Responsiveness – Response to customers and prompt service

Table 13.5	Principles of Service Design
Customer contact	How much contact is there between organisation and customer during service
Service mix	How many service offerings will there be. What is the service portfolio
Location	Should the service go to the customer or the customer to the service
Design	Design extend to interior design, uniforms, logos and literature
Technology	What technology is required to deliver the service. Is it reliable? What will be the customer experience?
Employees	Effective delivery will depend on the right employees, training, culture and internal marketing supported with adequate resources
Structure	The structure will influence the organisational culture and establishes the chain of command and the communication channels
Information	A good MIS system is essential for maintaining the appropriate levels of information to support service delivery. A good MKIS system will be essential to understanding customer expectations
Demand	Demand will effect the standards of delivery, therefore plan for peaks (add contingency)
Procedures	Analyse the procedures, understand what procedures are essential for excellence in service delivery
Control	Continuous improvement will only be achieved through monitoring and control and learning

3. Assurance – Knowledge and courtesy of employees, ability to inspire trust and confidence
4. Empathy – Caring, individual attention to customers
5. Tangibles – Physical facilities, quality of equipment appearance of personnel

SERVQUAL measures the gap between customer and management perceptions of quality.

The gaps are as follows:

Gap 1 – Consumers' expectations compared to managers' perceptions of consumer expectations

Gap 2 – Managers' perceptions of consumers' expectations compared to service quality specifications actually set

Gap 3 – Service quality specifications compared to actual service delivery

Gap 4 – Actual service delivery compared to external communications about the service

Gap 5 – Resources

Service quality is based on the three key service elements of the marketing mix: people, physical evidence and processes. Analysing the performance in these key areas, using SERVQUAL, will help the organisation to understand their position from a customer perspective and a competitive perspective.

Quality can be used as a useful tool for competitive advantage.

Developing a quality culture will require the organisation to look at the following key areas within an organisation.

- Leadership
- Values
- Rewards
- Empowerment of employees
- Development of a learning organisation

To be able to continuously improve the level of service offered, the monitoring and evaluation processes could be used, which are shown in Table 13.6.

Table 13.6	Methods of Monitoring Customer Service	
Customer satisfaction surveys	Performance appraisals
Mystery shopper survey	Employee discussions
Evaluation of complaints	Observation of customers

MARKETING PLANNING IN SMES

In 1996, the European Commission adopted the definitions of SMEs, which are shown in Table 13.7.

Table 13.7 Definitions of SMEs			
Maximum	**Microenterprise**	**Small**	**Medium sized**
Number of employees	10	50	250
Turnover (million Euro)	n/a	7	40
Balance sheet total (million Euro)	n/a	5	27

The term small and medium enterprises covers a wide range of businesses from sole trader enterprises through to businesses with sales of several million.

It is widely accepted that SMEs have different characteristics from larger companies. Schollhammer and Kuriloff (1979) summarised these as:

- Scope of operations
- Scale of operations
- Ownership
- Independence
- Management style

Entrepreneurial characteristics and activities impact on marketing activities in SMEs. This entrepreneurial marketing has a distinctive marketing style which is often characterised as shown in the Table 13.8.

Table 13.8 Characteristics of Entrepreneurial Marketing	
The Stage of development of the firms	Young firms will have simple marketing whereas the mature SME may have quite sophisticated marketing
Size of the firm	The stage of development, the size of the firm and limited resources will restrict marketing activity
Informal	SMEs do not have formal structures or communication structures
Simplistic and erratic	The influence of the entrepreneur, the size and lack of resources means *ad hoc* marketing takes place
Reactive	Reactive rather than proactive. Marketing tends to react to competitors' activity
Opportunistic	SME advantage is ability to react quickly to new opportunities, innovations and seize opportunities as they occur
Short term	SMEs decision-making is mostly short term

These characteristics, once recognised and understood, should be exploited in the preparation of marketing plans.

A business plan is essential for businesses applying for loans and grants or seeking outside investors and this is the only time many SMEs engage in planning activities. Many entrepreneurs object to preparing plans because they feel their time is better spent actively pursuing their business interests. The marketing plan is an integral part of any business plan. Marketing planning is basically a logical sequence of activities which lead to the setting of marketing objectives and the formulation of plans for achieving them. In major companies, there is usually a systemised management process followed in the preparation of plans, but in SMEs, the process is quite often informal.

- Identifying things the business was not aware of
- Identifying the strength and weaknesses of the business
- Identifying opportunities and threats
- Identifying critical success factors
- Setting out clear objectives

In many small businesses, the failure to research the market and prepare business and marketing plans result in a failure to achieve sales targets, poor profitability and cash flow problems. The business failure rate among SMEs is high with many failing in the first five years. A real understanding of the market and an effective marketing strategy is essential for the survival and growth of SMEs.

It is advisable for both the business plan and the marketing plan to be monitored on regular basis to establish whether targets and objectives are being achieved and to take corrective action if not.

SMEs, however, are often constrained in their marketing by limitations of financial resources and also the skills of marketing. Yet, it is important whenever possible to see expenditure on planning marketing as an investment in the future of the business rather than a cost.

The Marketing Mix for SMEs

Place

Many small and medium-sized manufacturing businesses concentrate on design and manufacture. Therefore, they rely on distributors to promote and sell products. These distributors will need to be incentivised to motivate them to work effectively for the businesses.

Price

These markets are often sensitive to price changes. Price wars and discounting can be a threat to SMEs, particularly those who do not have substantial financial resources. Attention to the breakeven point is essential to those businesses and close attention to profit margins is critical. Where discounts are necessary, these should be for regular customers or to encourage larger orders.

Promotion

Sales promotion in SMEs involves generating an awareness of the company and its products. Close communication with customers and potential customers is essential. Limited budgets will require close attention to the effectiveness of promotions.

Typical forms of promotion used by SMEs are:

- Yellow pages
- Direct marketing
- Internet
- Exhibitions
- Magazines
- Local radio
- Direct selling

MARKETING PLANNING FOR NOT FOR PROFIT

> An organisation whose prime goal is non-economic. However, it may undertake profit-making activities in pursuit of that prime goal.

The major difference between profit-making and non-profit-making businesses is the aims and objectives they pursue. The objective of commercial profit-making organizations is to maximise the profits and therefore the wealth of the owners or shareholders. Not-for-profit organizations, like charities have aims and objectives such as... 'To serve the needs of clients'

Marketing planning is as important to charities and other not-for-profit organizations as it is to major commercial ventures. The board or trustees of a charity or other not-for-profit organisation is composed of professionals who are responsible for the strategy and the effectiveness of the organization in meeting its prime goals. The board will set the objectives, develop strategy, utilize the resources, allocate funds and oversee any commercial profit-making activities the charity may develop.

There are many different sources of funds for not-for-profit organisations. Government grants, lottery funds, trust funds, donations and corporate funds from major companies.

The organisations may also receive the profits from profit-making activities such as charity shops.

Charities

The objectives of charities will reflect the constitution of the charity, with many having the objective of 'improving lives'. Objectives are likely to include creating awareness, generation of surplus funds, whereas another might be to generate those funds at a lower cost of administration.

The strategy should include the charity considering how it can retain some form of competitive advantage over other similar organisations. This should be considered not only in terms of funds raised but also in terms of attracting support from volunteers.

Marketing Segmentation and Targeting

Marketing segmentation consists of closely targeting individuals who are able to support the charity in various ways.

The key target audiences are:

- Donors – Those who provide funds or other support
- Clients – Those who are the users of the charitable donations
- Volunteers – Those who give time and effort to support the charity

Charity marketing usually has to offer some benefit, hence the flag days – where the donor gets a flag – as physical evidence of the support given by the donation.

The Marketing Mix

Product

This is the benefit the charity provides to donors, which may be just a feeling of well-being.

Place

Many charities run shops which raise significant funds.

Promotion

Public relations, sponsorship and promotions play a significant part. There is an increasing use of direct marketing to gain support and donations.

Price

The amount of money generated and the cost of the programme.

People

These are critical as many interact with the public.

Physical Evidence

Quality literature setting out how the money has been used.

Process

Making it easy to donate money. Solicitors supporting the charity will offer a free will service to those willing to donate from their will.

Implementation and Control

Controls will be based around the services mix to ensure quality of services are maintained. There is also likely to be financial controls monitoring the funds generated and the distribution of these to 'good causes'.

ACTIVITY 13.4

Choose a charity. Identify the three most important audiences which charities need to target? Why are they so important?

Charities are not the only form of not-for-profit organisation. The following are classified similarly due to their goals being essentially non-profit making, although they may be seeking commercial outcomes from their operation.

- Colleges and Universities
- Hospitals
- Medical practices
- Social organisations

Another group of important not-for-profit marketing organisations are public bodies such as government departments, agencies and local authorities. In the UK, these have become increasingly more goal oriented and have used marketing plans to achieve this. Some good examples include campaigns to promote healthy living, through reducing smoking and alcohol consumption, increasing physical exercise and encouraging better diets.

THE INTERNATIONAL AND GLOBAL DIMENSION OF MARKETING PLANNING

Although the key principles domestic marketing and international marketing remain the same, there are some factors that need to be taken into account when undertaking marketing planning in an international context, compared with marketing a single country situation (Table 13.9).

Table 13.9	Differences between Domestic and International Marketing
Domestic marketing	**International marketing**
Single dominant language	Many languages
Dominant culture	Multi-culture
Market research quite straightforward	Market research more complex
Relatively stable environment	Relatively unstable environment
Single currency	Exchange rate risks
Low-political risk	Political risk
Business conventions clear	Business conventions very diverse

Given the more complex nature of international marketing, why do organisations take the decision to move into new country markets?

- Intensity of the competition – There may be less competition overseas

- A saturated domestic market – Exploring market growth and development elsewhere

- Excess capacity – Excess capacity may be available to produce goods for other markets

- Product life cycle differences – Opportunities for products overseas at different stages of life cycle

- Financial reasons – Possible investment incentives not available for home market

- Organisational issues – Mergers and acquisitions may bring opportunities overseas

- Geographical diversification – To avoid intense competition, organisations may expand into new areas to diversify risk

- The decision to exploit international marketing opportunities will be a strategic one.

There are various levels of international marketing.

- Domestic/regional marketing – An example would be trading with the regional market of Europe.

- Export marketing – Where an organisation trades in goods and services across national boundaries. There are two types, direct and indirect.
  1. Direct exporting– Where goods and services are sold direct to customers in overseas market.

2. Indirect – Where with limited resources the organisation uses various market entry methods such as agents or export house.

- International marketing – Operating in a range of different markets with significant differences between markets. The controllable variables such as distribution networks, advertising and costs will also vary.

- Global marketing management – A more complex international operation. An integrated global effort, taking advantage of opportunities, exchange rates, different tax rates and labour rates.

Market Entry Strategies

Once the decision has been made to enter international markets, various ways of achieving this can be adopted.

Agents

Agents are effectively overseas sales personnel, who operate on behalf of different client organisations. Agents normally work on a retainer with additional commission or on commission only.

Licensing

Licensing is based on a contract that permits another party to produce products or services. This method of market entry requires low levels of investment.

Advantages are reduced market entry costs but contact may commit the organisation to long-term relationship.

Franchising

This is a very common method of market entry. Franchising requires franchisees to provide capital which makes this mode of entry cost effective for the franchisor. There are many examples of successful franchising, McDonalds, Pizza Hut and Body Shop.

Acquisitions

Gaining market entry through the acquisition of an organisation in the country in which you want to trade. This is a fast mode of entry because an established business is acquired. However, this mode of entry is high risk, requiring very careful research and due diligence.

Wholly Owned Subsidiary

One of the most expensive modes of entry, which requires substantial amounts of capital, is to set-up the organisation overseas.

Joint Ventures

Instead of setting up a wholly owned subsidiary, a joint venture can be established. The venture may be based on technological know-how, access to distribution network or for a competitive reason. There are many advantages including shared market research, shared product development, reduced capital and possibly less political risk. However, there may be conflict and trust, shared aims and objectives and strategies are essential.

Barriers to Entry

Sometimes difficulties exist that hinder the ability of a business to expand internationally.

Barker and Kaynak (1992) identified the following as potential barriers to entering new international markets:

- Trade barriers
- Language barriers
- Lack of competitive products
- Transportation difficulties
- Slow payment by buyers
- Red tape (bureaucracy)

The more informed the organisation, the clearer the country profile, the easier it will be to identify the best method for the organisation.

The Implications for International Marketing Plans

Product

New products for international markets will need to go through the same screening process used in the product development process for domestic markets. Screening should consider the following factors as outlined in Table 13.10.

Organisations will also need to consider the issue of branding. Will the brand be meaningful in the country they wish to operate in?

Table 13.10	Screening Factors for International NPD	
Customer needs and wants	Customer expectations
Standardized or adaptation	International (and local) safety standards
Fit with product portfolio	Capability of potential buyers to purchase
Patent and trade mark agreements	Technology demands
Technical support	After sales support

Pricing

The pricing of products is a greater challenge than domestic markets. Consideration must be given to the economic indicators and economic situation of the host country. Major influences will be local legislation, tariffs, tax rates, currency movements as well as the costs of manufacture and distribution. Credit terms, method of payment and speed of payment will be critical issues to consider when setting prices.

Price sensitivity will vary from country to country and pricing policy will be critical to obtaining and sustaining competitive positioning and market share. A significant implication will be that cultural diversity will have a large influence on the perceived value proposition.

Place

There are many logistical challenges with distribution. The selection of an appropriate market entry strategy will influence the way in which distribution can be effectively managed.

Management of channel members will require serious consideration. The following points should be borne in mind:

- Set-up costs of the channel and members
- Level of investment required
- Level of incentive
- Synergy with local/domestic channels
- Management and control of the overall process

The growth of the Internet is changing the dynamics of distribution and many organisations now deal on a more direct basis with customers overseas via the Internet, leading to a reduced role for distributors.

Promotional Mix

This area is challenging and complex area for the marketing planner. The characteristics and cultural differences will differ between countries and the factors influencing international promotion must be considered Table 13.11.

Internationalisation involves selling products across borders and trade increases at an international level. Globalisation is when there is not only an increase in the volume and value of goods exchanged internationally, but where there is:

- Transnational segments of consumers emerging
- Global brands are promoted worldwide
- Increased interdependence of international business

Table 13.11	Factors influencing International Promotion
Culture	Tolerance of advertising
Language	Advertising methods
Product range	Available advertising media
Product image	Use of agencies
Packaging	Literacy levels
Literature	Relationships
Corporate identity	Marketing ethics

The key success factor in achieving any marketing strategy, including globalisation, is to ensure that the organisation keeps a constant watch on the global marketing environment. Organisations should monitor changes and identify strengths, weaknesses, opportunities and threats.

Standardization Versus Adaptation

Globalisation is often characterised by the standardisation of the marketing mix. Alternatively marketers may plan to adapt the marketing effort to local market conditions. Standardisation is cost-effective and a very efficient approach, but it may not be the most competitive.

An organisation seeking to globalise would need to consider standardizing some or all of the following elements of its marketing:

- Market access
- Products
- Promotion
- Distribution
- Communications
- Services
- Technology
- Approach to competition

The marketing planner needs to remember that moving towards a standardised marketing mix will not guarantee success across all markets.

Adaptation means that part or even the whole of the marketing mix has to be changed to meet the changing needs of different countries.

An adaptation of the *product* involves many companies changing their products to meet local needs and conditions, and organisations will either adapt or change the *promotional* strategies. The names of products can cause conflict and misunderstanding so may need to be changed.

Price can be used to position the product accordingly in the market to take account of its perceived value that may be delivered through the brand. Pricing must however take account of local factors such as the costs of production, exchange rates, disposable income, taxes amongst other things. Similarly *place* may change depending on the factors that affect distribution such as market accessibility and the structure of retailing.

The ultimate decision whether to standardize or to adapt products can only be based upon knowledge and a wide range of information about each foreign market, its characteristics, cultures and channels.

MARKETING PLANNING FOR THE VIRTUAL MARKETPLACE

The Internet has changed the way we do business. It is no longer necessary to have face-to-face contact with a sales person or supplier. The 'pure' Internet companies have created strong online brand recognition, provided good customer service and are open 24 hours a day, 7 days a week and 365 days per year. The ability to customise service allows these organizations to develop a relationship with their customers. The Internet has made substantial inroads into both the B2C and B2B markets and online business is forecast to be the biggest growth area of the next decade. Traditional companies, often referred to as bricks and mortars (B&Ms) have been pressurised to respond to the competitive threat from both 'pure' e-businesses and the traditional companies that have added e-business activities.

Key trends in the virtual marketing environment are:

- Convergence of technologies
- Development of digital technologies
- Consumer time poverty
- Consumers looking to take control

Marketing via the Internet has increased dramatically over the last 15 years. Marketing planners need to consider how best to incorporate this medium into their planning.

The Internet can be used in many ways to support marketing activities:

- Online sales – Online catalogues and purchases
- Promotion – Advertising banners on websites
- Customer service – Provision of customer information via the Internet
- Public relations – Channel for news
- Marketing research – Collection of detailed information from websites for customer profiling which can be added to databases.

Evans and Wurster (2000) identified three bases of competitive advantage.

1. Reach – Referring to access and connection
2. Richness – Referring to detail and depth of information to customers
3. Affiliation – Referring to whose interests the business represents

These bases need to be considered when planning. Technology is converging and more organisations are using digital marketing to reach and retain customers, i.e. to attract customers initially and build and manage relationships with them.

Mobile marketing is also growing in its usage with digital information, such as videos, text messages, voice messages are sent to mobiles.

Companies can benefit from embracing blogging and utilising it as a marketing tool. A blog on a company website enables a wide audience to be reached.

According to Wright (2006), companies blogging is about three things:

1. Information – Telling your customers what you are doing and finding out what they think

2. Relationships – Building a solid base of positive experiences with customers

3. Knowledge management – Obtaining and communicating knowledge within the organization to the right people at the right time

Blogging enables a company to obtain valuable information about the types of customers that are buying products and services. Instant qualitative information about customers and ideas to improve products and services can be obtained without the expense associated with market research.

Marketing planning in virtual environments needs to take account of the way that consumer behaviour is changing with regard to new information and communications technologies and how they are being used to achieve a competitive advantage.

QUESTIONS

1. Distinguish between the key characteristics of B2B and B2C markets and how this influences differences in marketing planning?

2. What are the unique characteristics of services? How do these translate into differences in marketing activity in practice between services and physical goods?

3. Who are the main audiences of public sector organisations? What are their different expectations and how can these be met through marketing plans?

SUMMARY

Marketing planning, implementation and control are intrinsically linked. Whether marketing planning is in a FMCG, B2B, services, SME, not-for-profit context the fundamentals remain the same. Similarly, the principles of marketing planning apply equally in international marketing as they do in domestic markets. However, a range of factors affect marketing planning in different settings and marketing mangers need to be aware of these when developing and implementing plans in different contexts.

BIBLIOGRAPHY

Barker, A. and Kaynak, E. (1992) An Empirical Investigation of the Differences between Initiating and Continuing Exporters. *European Journal of Marketing*, 26(3), 27–36.

Dibb, S., Simkin, L., Pride, W. and Ferrell, O.C. (2006) *Marketing: Concepts and Strategies*, 5th edition. Houghton Mifflin, Boston.

Evans, P.B. and Wurster, T.S. (2000) *Blown to Bits: How the New Economics of Information Transforms Strategy*. Harvard Business School Press, Boston.

Mudie, P. and Cottam, A. (1999) *The Management and Marketing of Services*, 2nd edition. Butterworth-Heinemann, Oxford.

Parasuraman, A., Berry, L.L. and Zeithaml, V.A. (1985) A Conceptual Model of Service Quality and Its Implications for Future Research. *Journal of Marketing*, 49(4), 41–50.

Schollhammer, H. and Kuriloff, A. (1979) *Entrepreneurship and Small Business Management*. John Wiley, New York.

Wright, J. (2006) *Blog Marketing: The Revolutionary New Way to Increase Sales, Profits and Growth*. McGraw Hill, New York.

Senior Examiner's Comments – Section Four

On completion of Section 4, students should have a detailed knowledge and understanding of:

- the dimensions of marketing planning implementation including, structures, systems, responsibilities, budgets, timescales, and monitoring and control procedures;

- the barriers to implementing marketing planning and plans;

- the ways in which ineffective marketing planning may be addressed;

- the range of contextual marketing planning situations that face different organisations in practice;

- the parameters of different marketing planning contexts that need to be taken account of when shaping detailed marketing plans to achieve organisational marketing objectives.

Candidates must be able to apply their understanding of implementation of marketing planning to different business and organisational settings. To achieve this, they should recognize that successful marketing planning and implementation of plans leading to desired results requires the right structures, internal systems, finance, monitoring and control mechanisms, and cultural determination to provide support to ensure that it happens.

It is important to find examples of good marketing planning leading to effective action and outcomes. However, students should also be aware that poor marketing and the ineffective implementation of plans can easily come about if barriers to planning are encountered such as limited resources and lack of support from senior management. Examples of these positive organisational characteristics as well shortcomings should be sought from outside the candidate's own organisation in addition to any they have encountered from their own experience.

Means of addressing barriers to planning should also be well understood and examples sought of how this may be undertaken through such initiatives as cultural change brought about by internal marketing. Particular implementation issues may be encountered in specialized marketing contexts which result from organisational characteristics or specific aspects of the markets served or products offered. It is important that students are familiar with such circumstances and seek illustrative examples of how relevant theory in such contexts is applied in practice. They also need to be able to evaluate how well this translates into reality and its effectiveness in achieving intended outcomes.

Index